Benni Harper's
Quilt Album

A Scrapbook of Quilt Projects,
Photos & Never-Before-Told Stories

EARLENE FOWLER
& MARGRIT HALL

C&T PUBLISHING

Text and Artwork © Earlene Fowler and Margrit Hall
Artwork © 2004 C&T Publishing, Inc.

Publisher: Amy Marson
Editorial Director: Gailen Runge
Acquisitions Editor: Jan Grigsby
Editor: Cyndy Lyle Rymer
Technical Editors: Carolyn Aune, Joyce Lytle
Copyeditor/Proofreader: Linda Dease Smith
Cover Designer: Christina D. Jarumay
Design Director/Book Designer: Christina D. Jarumay
Illustrator: Mary Ann Tenorio
Production Assistants: Kirstie L. McCormick, Kerry Graham
Photography: Quilts by Sharon Risedorph, location shots by Allen Fowler and David Hall,
cover by Diane Pedersen, styled by Diane Pedersen and Jan Grigsby
Published by C&T Publishing, Inc., P.O. Box 1456, Lafayette, California 94549

Front cover: *It's Never Too Late to Be a Cowgirl*, Margrit Hall and Tami Taylor
Back cover: *Coming Storms*, Margrit Hall and Cathryn Tallman-Evans

Attention Copy Shops: Please note the following exception—Publisher and author give
permission to photocopy pages 31, 41, 69, 89, and the pullout for personal use only.

Attention Teachers: C&T Publishing, Inc. encourages you to use this book as a text for
teaching. Contact us at 800-284-1114 or www.ctpub.com for more information about the
C&T Teachers Program.

We take great care to ensure that the information included in this book is accurate and
presented in good faith, but no warranty is provided nor results guaranteed. Having no
control over the choices of materials or procedures used, neither the author nor C&T
Publishing, Inc. shall have any liability to any person or entity with respect to any loss or
damage caused directly or indirectly by the information contained in this book. For your
convenience, we post an up-to-date listing of corrections on our web page (www.ctpub.com).
If a correction is not already noted, please contact our customer service department at
ctinfo@ctpub.com or at P.O. Box 1456, Lafayette, California 94549.

Trademarked (™) and Registered Trademark (®) names are used throughout this book.
Rather than use the symbols with every occurrence of a trademark and registered trademark name, we are using the names only in the editorial fashion and to
the benefit of the owner, with no intention of infringement.

Library of Congress Cataloging-in-Publication Data
Fowler, Earlene.
  Benni Harper's quilt album : a scrapbook of quilt projects,
photos & never-before-told stories / Earlene Fowler & Margrit Hall.
      p. cm.
  Includes bibliographical references and index.
  ISBN 1-57120-244-7 (paper trade)
  1. Patchwork--Patterns. 2. Quilting. 3. Harper, Benni (Fictitious
character--Fiction. 4. Quilting--Fiction. 5. Quilts--Fiction. I. Hall,
Margrit. II. Title.

TT835.F69 2004
746.46'041--dc22

                                        2004008152

Printed in China
10 9 8 7 6 5 4 3 2 1

Dedications

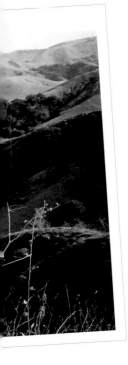

To all the fans and friends of Benni Harper and her extended family in San Celina. Thank you for your incredible support and enthusiasm.

With love to my husband, Allen, who, without question, took pictures for this book of whatever I pointed to and who was always up for a "road trip," no matter how tired he was.

Earlene

To my husband and best friend, David, for his love, help, and encouragement, and to my children, Valerie, Robyn, and Eric, who grew up thinking that playing under a quilt frame was perfectly normal.

Margrit

Acknowledgments

We give heartfelt thanks to Ginny Jaranowski, Rhoda Nelson, and Cathryn Tallman-Evans, fabulous quilters who went above and beyond the call of friendship.

We also sincerely thank all the incredible quilters who gave of their time and talents: Elaine Denham, Kelly Gallagher-Abbott, Vicki Hoskins, Robyn Malone, Kathleen Pappas, Judy Rhodes, and Tami Taylor.

A special thank you to Phyllis Reddish for her almost superhuman ability to quilt a project overnight!

Thanks to our agent, Ellen Geiger, for her hard work and expertise.

Thank you to C&T editors Jan Grigsby and Joyce Lytle for being the first people to make contact about this book. Their enthusiasm and persistence is why this book became a reality.

Thank you to our C&T editors, Cyndy Lyle Rymer and Carolyn Aune, for their dedication to making this book special.

A great big Western thank you to all the fine folks at C&T Publishing for their hospitality and devotion to making beautiful quilt books for all of us to enjoy. We had a great time working with you all!

Thank you to Superior Threads for their contribution of the thread for all of the quilt projects, and to The Fabric Patch of Montclair, CA quilt shop, Hoffman California Fabrics, Robert Kaufman Fabric Co., Rainbow Fabrics, and Timeless Treasures Fabric Co. for their donations of the fabric used in the quilts.

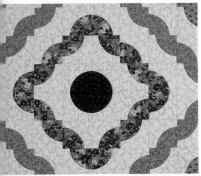

TABLE OF

CONTENTS

The Real Story
Behind the Quilts

People often ask me why I chose quilts as the theme for my mystery series. When I started the first Benni Harper novel thirteen years ago, I have to admit I had no idea there were so many quilters in the world. I simply wanted to write quilts into my story because I love their colors, their artistry, the stories behind them. And I've always been fascinated by the women who make them.

I didn't grow up with quilts. In my house, in the suburbs of Southern California, my mother never owned anything except store-bought blankets. She grew up a sharecropper's child during the Depression 1930s in southwestern Arkansas. Like many women with similar backgrounds, she associated anything handmade with being poor. But when I visited her mother, my Grandma Webb, my sisters and I would be tucked away under the most brilliantly colored and patterned quilts. I think it was then that my love for quilts began. When I attended quilt shows, I always wondered about the women who made them—why they picked a particular pattern, who they were making the quilt for, what was happening in their lives when they stitched the quilt into existence.

I started writing when I was twenty-seven years old, but none of my writing included quilts until I wrote my first novel ten years later. I was halfway through *Fool's Puzzle*, the plot of which centered around a quilt show at a folk art museum, when the idea of naming my book after a quilt pattern came to me. I was at a quilt show looking at the beautiful quilts when it occurred to me that quilt patterns had evocative names, names that suggested stories. I titled my first book after a quilt, thinking that first, it would be the only book about these characters I would ever write, and second, like most first novels, it probably would never be published. I took my almost-finished novel to a writing class at a local community college. When I turned in my first chapter, Jo-Ann Mapson, the teacher and a writer herself, asked to see the entire manuscript. She liked it and said she wanted to show it to her agent in New York. She asked me if I had an idea for a series and suggested perhaps that the concept was something I should put in my query letter. Since I'm horrible at thinking up titles, I immediately said, "How about quilt patterns?" With that statement, the Benni Harper quilt-titled mystery series was born.

■ This truck has traveled many miles with me during research for my novels. Many of my rancher friends, who believe that any color of truck other than white is too flashy, find my city-girl truck amusing.

■ When I bought my purple pickup truck, I really wanted boots that matched. It took me eight years, but I finally found them!

Although quilts are definitely a part of my series and of Benni's life, they had always been meant to serve as a metaphor for the stories, sometimes even as a way for the stories to be told, just like real quilts do in people's lives.

It was also at a quilt show that it occurred to me that quilts are things that bind women together in a very fundamental way. Even if they have never threaded a needle in their lives, or intend to, most women cannot walk by a handmade quilt without stopping to marvel at its beauty and artistry. Something in quilts speaks to women and connects us, erasing everything that is different and highlighting everything that is the same.

It was quite early in my series that I started contemplating a book of quilt patterns based on my books. After my second book, *Irish Chain*, came out, I was signing books at one of my local quilt stores, The Fabric Patch, during a "Meet the Teachers" day. Sitting across from me was a quilt teacher and designer named Margrit Hall. I was immediately drawn to her work. Her quilts reminded me of my novels because her specialty was using traditional patterns in untraditional ways, which is just how I've tried to write my novels. We started talking and found we had a rapport—she obviously loved quilts and

liked my books, and she'd grown up in Wyoming and was able to relate to the Western flavor of my novels. We met for lunch a few times and once had dinner together with our husbands. It was at dinner that I brought up the idea of a book of patterns. She thought it was a wonderful idea. But, as often is the case, life and all its problems intervened. She was busy teaching classes, designing quilts, and working as curator for the Hoffman Challenge. I was on a book-a-year schedule that left little time to do much but write and promote my books. Flash forward six years. We stayed in casual contact, and during one phone call, I brought up the quilt pattern book again. For some reason, though I'd had many offers, I'd always known Margrit was the right person to bring my fictional quilts to life. Many of the themes in my novels have dealt with things in life working out in their own time, with my belief that there is a plan for our lives. Such was definitely the case with this book. Margrit and I met a couple of times at a coffeehouse halfway between our homes (she lives about twenty miles from me) to discuss what kind of book we both envisioned. Then one day I was contacted by C&T Publishing about working on a pattern book based on my series.

■ Margrit and I used to meet at a coffeehouse halfway between our homes (we live about twenty miles apart). There were two chairs we thought of as "ours," and it was disconcerting when someone else was sitting in them!

■ Husbands/photographers, Allen and David

■ Margrit and I in our coffeehouse again. Our husbands were trying to take candid pictures and finding it impossible (neither Margrit nor I like our pictures taken). Once we started actually talking about the book, they caught this picture of us.

"Funny you should bring it up," I wrote them. "I have an idea for a book and the perfect quilt designer in mind."

I told C&T that I wanted this to be a special book for my fans and that it should be accessible to all of them, not just the quilters. Maybe it would entice some nonquilters into trying quilting!

"I want to write original stories for this book," I told them. "Scenes that happen offstage, such as Benni and Gabe's wedding. Margrit will design quilts to fit the books and these new scenes." C&T liked the idea, and in that moment, *Benni Harper's Quilt Album* started to become a reality.

Margrit and I have had great fun collaborating. There have been innumerable meetings at our coffee-house and our homes, some trips to fabric companies, road trips to C&T and San Luis Obispo (the town on which I have based San Celina), and many long phone conversations when she or I were creatively blocked or just needed to "talk out" our creative challenges. Our dear husbands, Allen and David, have good-

naturedly suffered along with us, and we both feel extremely blessed to have them in our lives.

So I offer up my stories and Margrit's quilts to you, my dear fans, with the hope that you will enjoy them. I am thankful to each of you for your enthusiasm and support throughout the years. As Dove would say, "Y'all have been real good company. Don't forget to come back and visit us again."

May your trails always be happy, with many colorful fabric stops along the way.

Earlene Fowler

■ Here's Margrit doing what she does best—designing beautiful and breathtaking quilts! This book has been an incredible adventure for both of us.

■ While Margrit is creating her quilts, I'm at home in my office (and my favorite chair) writing about Benni, Gabe, and all the folks in San Celina.

■ Margrit and I at her studio going over the original quilt top for the *Señor Azure* quilt.

Character
BIOGRAPHIES

Albenia "Benni" Harper A thirty-four-year-old widowed rancher who also works as a curator of the local folk art museum and artists' co-op. She grew up in the college and agricultural town of San Celina on California's central coast. Although she was born in Arkansas, she has lived in San Celina most of her life.

Gabriel "Gabe" Ortiz San Celina's newly appointed police chief. He is forty-two, has dazzling blue eyes, is part Hispanic and part Anglo, and was born in Derby, Kansas. He and Benni have a contentious and passionate relationship.

Dove Ramsey Benni's seventy-five-year-old grandmother from Sugartree, Arkansas. She came to live in San Celina when Benni's mother died when Benni was six years old. Dove rules the roost at the Ramsey Ranch. She is barely five feet tall and has long white hair that she wears in a single thick braid.

Ben Ramsey Benni's father and Dove's oldest son. A respected local rancher, Ben epitomizes the silent, hardworking Western man.

Elvia Aragon Benni's best friend since they were both in second grade. She is the oldest of seven children and the only daughter. She owns Blind Harry's Bookstore in San Celina.

Emory Littleton Benni's handsome and smooth-talking cousin from Sugartree, Arkansas. He is a year younger than her and, next to Elvia, is her best friend. His father owns a smoked-chicken business in Sugartree.

Garnet Wilcox Dove's younger sister who lives in Sugartree, Arkansas. They have always been in competition for everything. Even though they love each other, they are exact opposites in clothing styles, personality, and life view.

With This Ring
Earlene Fowler

Dearly Beloved: We are gathered together this day in the sight of God and His angels, with friends and loved ones, to unite this man, Gabriel Ortiz, and this woman, Albenia Harper, in holy matrimony, which is an honorable estate . . .

What am I thinking? I don't even know this man! What has it been, three months? He could be a serial killer for all I know. Wait, now calm down. He's the chief of police, for crying out loud. Surely the San Celina City Council did a background check on him. Maybe I should have done one of my own. I mean, what do I really know about him? He says he's from Kansas, has two sisters, a mother who's a teacher, a dad who died when Gabe was sixteen. He says he was a Marine in Vietnam. Well, that part seems believable. I've never seen a speck of dirt on his shoes. I hope he doesn't expect me to be that spick-and-span. Oh, he's good-looking, there's no doubt about that. Those eyes. Those incredible blue-gray eyes pinned me to the ground the first moment I saw him. He probably knew that too. I mean, you know the man's had a gazillion women in his life. How in the world can I live up to that? And he's been married before. I don't even really know what broke up his first marriage. This is crazy. My gramma Dove is

going to kill me dead when she finds out we eloped. And to Las Vegas! Why did I let him talk me into getting married here? Is this minister even for real? And this chapel, Wee Kirk O' the Heather, what kind of name is that for a wedding chapel? Neither of us is even Scottish. Is it my imagination, or does that minister look a little like Elvis? But Gabe arranged it and the chapel is real pretty and those eyes. The way they're looking at me right now, I'd go anywhere . . .

Let us remember what is said in First Corinthians 13, "Love bears all things, believes all things, hopes all things, and endures all things. Love never ends . . ."

I wish my mother were here. This is the second wedding of mine she has missed. Oh, how I long for her sometimes. Even if I can barely remember her face or her voice or how she smells. Six years old. That is just too young to lose your mother. Can she see me? All those country-western songs are always saying that, claiming those who died can look down on us and observe our lives. I'm not sure I believe that. If there's no sadness in heaven, which is what they always tell us, wouldn't that be enough to make you sad, seeing the daughter you didn't get to raise getting married again? I like the idea of her watching though. If you are there Mama, what do you think? Is Gabe a good man?

■ Vineyards are prominent everywhere in the county now.

■ I took this picture sitting in the back of a pickup truck being driven by a ranch hand. I was throwing hay off the back to lure the cattle back to the barn to be vaccinated and tagged.

As good as Jack was? Are you and Jack sitting next to each other on a heavenly front porch watching me jump the broomstick? Tell me, what do you see in my future? Is it true that love never ends? Will Gabe and I have that kind of love? What if we don't? What if this feeling is just an illusion, a trick of hormones, a wisp of passion? What if he dies before me? Should I even take that chance again?

I, Gabriel Thomas Ortiz, do take you, Albenia Louise Harper, to be my beloved wife, from this day forward, to honor, cherish and protect you, forsaking all others before you, in sickness and in health, for richer or poorer, until death do us part. Before God, this is my solemn vow . . .

He does look so incredibly solemn. He is a serious man, there's no doubt about that, though no one since Jack has ever made me laugh like Gabe. Not many people see that playful part of him. Joe Friday, I still call him. But he knows it's no longer in derision. I am so in love with this man I sometimes feel sick. Does he feel the same way? With Jack, our love was so even, so balanced. But this man, oh, this man. He grips my soul in a way that Jack never did. I'm sorry, Jack. You were my first love, my dear, sweet first love. No one will ever take your place in my life. But this man has seared my heart. You were the love of my youth, but he is the love of my life. But what if . . . what if I'm not the love of his? What am I doing? Maybe I should run while I can. I saw a car rental place across the street . . .

With this ring, I thee wed...

I love the feel of his strong hands. They are not the hands of a man who shuffles papers, though that's all he claims he does as a police chief. These calloused, capable hands I am holding are of someone who can fix an engine, repair a sink, control a horse, hold a woman with passion. He will be a good lover. His kisses steal the very life from me. When his hands touch me, I swear my skin burns. But will that be enough? Can I trust those same hands that hold my face with such tenderness to hold me when I am dying? I trust his hands, but can I trust his heart?

What God has joined together, let no man put asunder. By the power entrusted to me by the state of Nevada, I now pronounce you husband and wife. Mr. Ortiz, you may kiss your bride.

Oh, his kiss! His kiss. I may be crazy, but it feels right, feels exactly right. This is the man I want to be with for the rest of my life. Before God, I declare this to be true.

"So, *querida*," he whispered seconds after our kiss, our lips still millimeters away from each other. "You still have time to run. Any doubts?"

I reached up and touched his cheek, feeling like my heart would burst. "Not a one, Friday. Not a single one."

■ Another view of the Rios-Caledonia Adobe in the town of San Miguel. The folk art museum was inspired by this building.

■ This is the Rios-Caledonia Adobe of San Miguel

■ Oak trees reign in San Luis Obispo County.

With This Ring

Designed by Margrit Hall

Appliquéd by Elaine Denham and Rhoda Nelson

Quilted by Phyllis Reddish

Finished Block Size: 13$\frac{1}{2}$"

Finished Quilt Size: 73$\frac{1}{4}$" x 73$\frac{1}{4}$"

Fabric graciously supplied by RJR Fabrics.

✳ FABRICS AND CUTTING

Template patterns are located on the pullout.

FABRIC COLOR	FABRIC AMOUNT	CUTTING DIRECTIONS
Cream Background	5¾ yards	Cut a piece 80" long x the width of the fabric from the total yardage, then cut into 4 lengthwise strips 7½" x 80" for 2nd border. Cut 2 squares 23¼" x 23¼", then cut each square once on the diagonal to make 4 triangles for corner sections. Cut 4 strips 3" wide for corner sections. Cut 8 strips 2¼" wide for binding. Cut 2 strips 12" wide, then cut into 8 F's and 4 G's for blocks. Cut 36 D's and 13 E's from the remaining fabric for blocks.
Green	1⅝ yards	Cut 2 strips 2" wide for center star. Cut 2 strips 1⅝" wide for corner stars. Cut 8 strips 1½" wide for corner sections. Cut 1 strip 21" wide, then cut in half to make 2 squares 21" x 21" for vines. Cut 104 H's for leaves.
Pink	⅜ yard	Cut 2 strips 2" wide for center star. Cut 2 strips 1⅝" wide for corner stars.
Blue	⅜ yard	Cut 3 strips 2" wide for center star. Cut 3 strips 1⅝" wide for corner stars.
Yellow	½ yard	Cut 3 strips 3" wide, then cut into 36 C's for blocks. Cut 1 strip 2" wide for center star. Cut 1 strip 1⅝" wide for corner stars. Cut 24 I's for circle flowers.
Purple	½ yard	Cut 3 strips 3" wide, then cut into 36 C's for blocks. Cut 1 strip 2" wide for center star. Cut 1 strip 1⅝" wide for corner stars.

12 Prints	⅜ yard **each** of 6 of the prints and ½ yard **each** of another 6 prints that are also used for circle flowers	Cut 1 strip 2¼" wide from each of 9 print fabrics.
		    Fold each strip in half, wrong sides together, and cut 8 pairs
		    of B's (8 B and 8 Br). Each cut equals 1 pair (72 total pairs).
		 Cut 2 strips 2¼" wide of each print, then cut 24 A's for blocks (288 total).
		 Cut 1 strip 2" wide from each print for 1st border.
		 Cut 24 J's from each of the 6 prints (144 total) for circle flowers.

Backing	4⅝ yards	Piece together.

Other materials: ¼" bias pressing bar, threads to match appliqué

Press seams in the direction of the arrows unless otherwise indicated.

✳ BLOCK ASSEMBLY

1. Using a random selection of fabrics, sew 4 A's together to make Unit A. Press the seams in one direction. Make 8 units for each block (72 total).

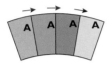

Unit A Make 8 units for each block.

2. Sew a B to the left side of Unit A and a B reverse to the right side of Unit A to make Unit B. Press. Make a total of 8 units for each block (72 total).

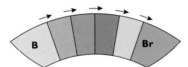

Unit B Make 8 units for each block.

3. Sew a purple C to the left side and a yellow C to the right side of half (36) of the Unit B's to make Unit C. Press. Make 4 units for each block (36 total).

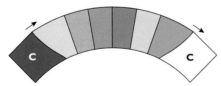

Unit C Make 4 units for each block.

4. Mark dots from patterns on D and the remaining half of the Unit B's. With right sides together, pin D's to Unit B's. Pin at the centers first, then the ends, and then place pins between.

5. Place Unit B on top and sew between the dots, backstitching at each end to make Unit D. Do not sew through the seam allowance. Press toward D. Make 4 units for each block (36 total).

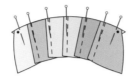

Pin and sew between the dots.

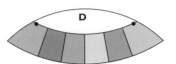

Unit D Make 4 units for each block.

6. With right sides together, sew Unit C's to Unit D's, with Unit C's on top. Sew between the dots, backstitching at each end (1). Do not sew through the seam allowance.

7. To complete Section 1, sew purple C's to Br's and yellow C's to B's (2 and 3). Sew to the dot and backstitch; do not sew through the seam allowance. Press toward Unit D. Make 4 sections for each block (36 total).

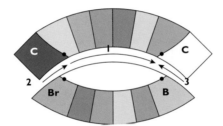

Sew between the dots.

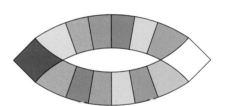

Section 1 Make 4 for each block.

8. Sew Section 1's to each side of E, alternating the positions of the yellow and purple C's. Sew between the dots, backstitching at each end.

9. Sew a yellow C to a purple C. Sew to the dot and backstitch. Repeat at each yellow and purple C to complete the block. Clip and press C seams open. Make 9 blocks.

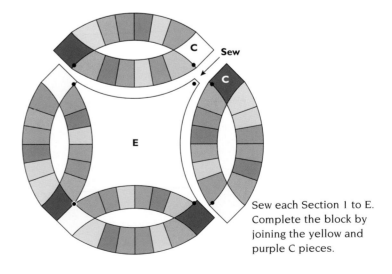

Sew each Section 1 to E. Complete the block by joining the yellow and purple C pieces.

QUILT CENTER ASSEMBLY

1. Sew blocks in diagonal rows, with the remaining E pieces between the blocks and the F side pieces or G corner pieces at the ends of the rows. Stitch between the dots and backstitch.
2. Carefully pin the rows together and sew. Clip at the seams of C pieces and press C seams open. Press the remainder of the seams toward the E or F pieces. Add the G corner pieces and press.

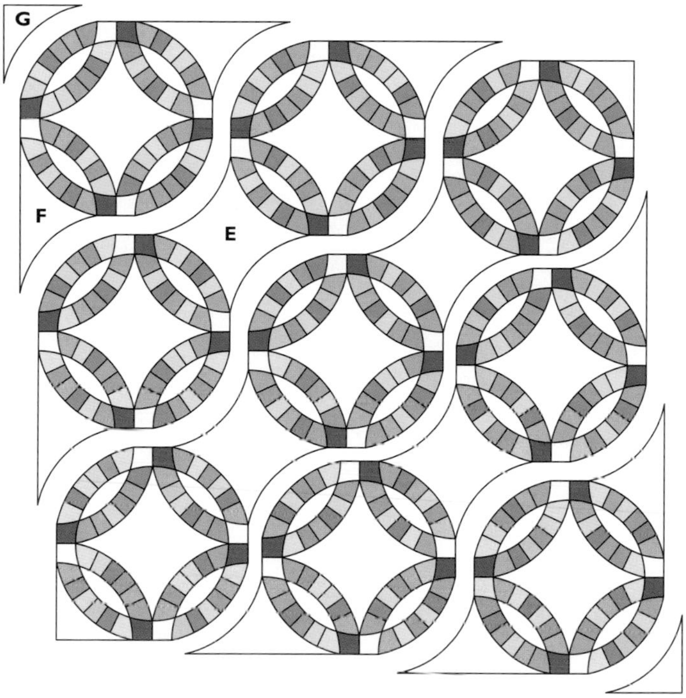

CENTER STAR ASSEMBLY

1. Sew together 2"-wide strips of green, pink, blue, yellow, or purple to make strip sets with the colors shown for each set. Offset the strips by approximately $2^1/_4$". Press.

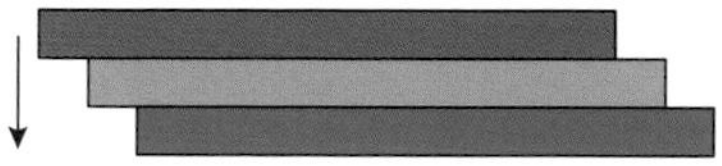

Set 1 Make 1.

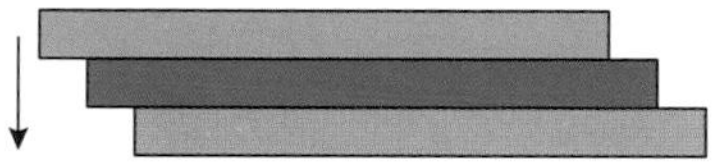

Set 2 Make 1.

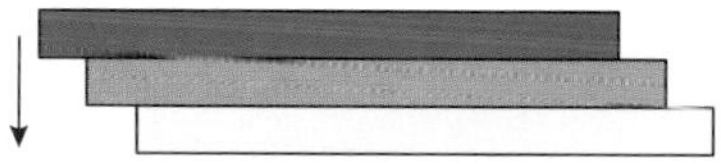

Set 3 Make 1.

2. Line up the 45° angle on the ruler with the edge of Set 1. Trim the edge.

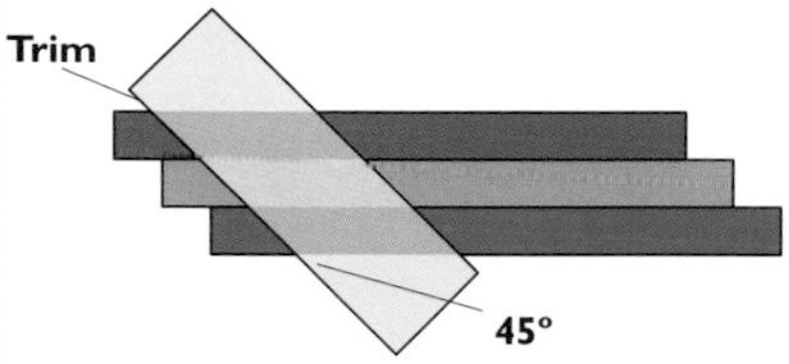

3. Cut Set 1 into 8 segments 2" wide. Repeat for Sets 2 and 3.

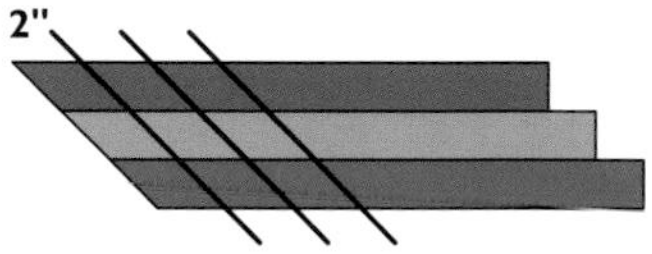

4. Carefully pin, matching the seams at the intersections, and sew together 1 segment each from Sets 1, 2, and 3 to make a star point. Make 8 points total. Press seams open.

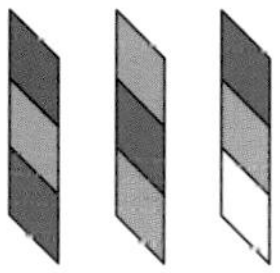

1 segment from each set.

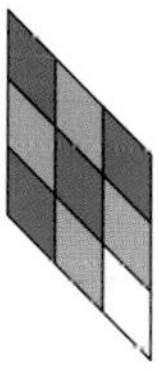

Star Point Make 8.

Hint

The seams of the diamond segments do not go in the same direction; they cross at the $^1/_4$" seam allowance. To make sure your seams match, pin each intersection where the corresponding seams meet.

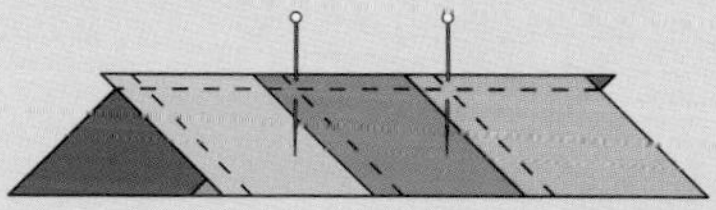

Pin and sew together.

5. Mark a dot ¼" in from the corner of each star point. Sew 2 star points together to make a quarter-star Unit A. Sew to the dot and backstitch. Make 4.

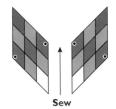

Quarter-Star Unit A Make 4.

6. To construct half-star units, sew 2 Unit A's together to make Unit B. Sew to the dot and backstitch. Make 2. Press seams open.

Half-Star Unit B Make 2.

7. Sew 2 Unit B's together to make the star, stitching between the dots and backstitching at each end. Press seams open.

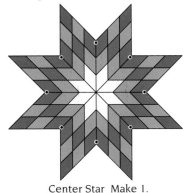

Center Star Make 1.

8. Draw a line ¼" in from the edge of the star points. Turn under on the line and press. Referring to the quilt photo on page 12 for placement, hand appliqué to the center of the quilt.

✳ CORNER HALF STAR ASSEMBLY

1. Follow Steps 1–3 of Center Star Assembly to make the corner half stars with the following changes: Use the 1⅝" wide strips of green, pink, blue, yellow, or purple to make 3 strip sets. Offset the strips by approximately 1¾", and cut into 16 segments 1⅝" wide.

2. Follow Steps 4–6 of Center Star Assembly to make Corner Half Star.

3. Draw a line ¼" from the edge of the star points; turn under and press.

4. Fold a 23¼" background triangle in half and crease at the center. Center the raw edge of the half-star unit along the diagonal edge. Hand appliqué to the background triangle.

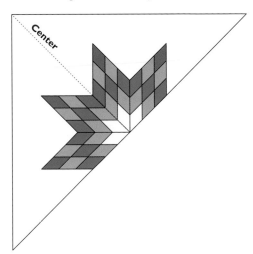

✳ CORNER SECTION ASSEMBLY

1. Sew 1½" green strips to both sides of a 3" background strip to make Unit A. Press.

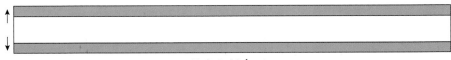

Unit A Make 4.

2. Mark the center of Unit A and match to the center of the half-star corner triangle.

3. Sew Unit A to the diagonal side of the half-star corner triangle. Press toward Unit A.

4. Lay a ruler along the top edge of the corner unit and trim Unit A even with the top edge of the corner triangle. Repeat for the side. Make 4 half-star corner units.

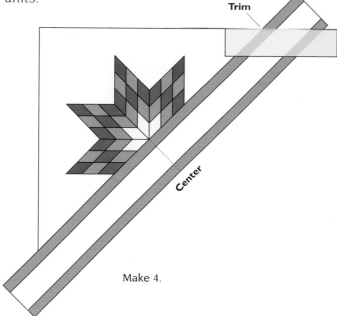

Make 4.

5. Match the center of the corner section and the center of each side of the center quilt section. Sew half-star corner sections to 2 opposite sides of the center quilt section, matching the centers. Press toward the corner section.

6. Sew half-star corner sections to the remaining 2 sides of the wedding ring square. Press.

QUILT ASSEMBLY

First Border

1. Sew 12 strips of 2"-wide print fabric together lengthwise. Press seams in one direction. Cut into 24 segments $1\frac{1}{2}$" wide.

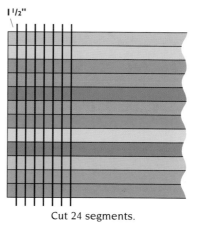

Cut 24 segments.

2. Sew 5 segments end-to-end to make one long strip for Border 1. Make 4 Border 1 strips.

3. Fold the segment strips in half to find the center. Press on the fold.

Second Border

1. Fold the 4 strips of $7\frac{1}{2}$" x 80" background fabric in half to find the center. Press on the fold.

2. Match the centers of Borders 1 and 2 and sew together.

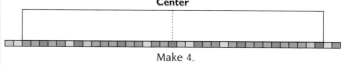

Center

Make 4.

3. Sew to quilt and miter borders, referring to Quilting Basics on page 90.

Appliqué

1. To make the bias strips for the appliquéd vine, fold each of the green 21" squares on the diagonal. Cut off the fold and cut into 1"-wide bias strips.

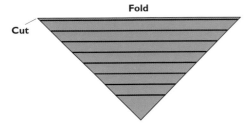

2. Lay bias strips right sides together, perpendicular to each other, and sew, using a $^1/_4$" seam. Press all seams in one direction. Continue to join enough strips to make 4 strips, each 85" long.

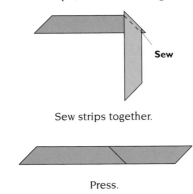

Sew strips together.

Press.

3. Fold strips in half lengthwise, right sides out. Stitch a scant $^1/_4$" from the raw edge. Trim the seam allowance.

4. Insert a $^1/_4$" bias bar into the bias tube and roll the seam to the center of the bias bar. Press as you slide the bias bar through the inside of the tube, centering the seam in the back of the tube.

Hint

Moving the bias bar along will be easier if you insert the bar so it passes through the tube in the same direction that the piecing seams are pressed.

5. Using your favorite appliqué method and the quilt photo on page 12 for placement, appliqué vine, flowers, and leaves to the border. Lay out the vine one side at a time, starting and ending at the corners. Trim excess vine at the corners. The corner flowers will cover the seam.

6. To make a circle flower, sew 6 J circles together. Make 24 flowers. Appliqué the flower to the quilt and add Center Circle I.

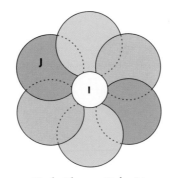

Circle Flower Make 24.

Hint

To make appliqué circles, cut a cardboard template to the actual size. Lay the template on the wrong side of the fabric and draw around it. Cut a generous $^1/_4$" away from the drawn line. Sew a running stitch $^1/_8$" away from the line. Replace the template, and pull the running stitch to gather the fabric around the template. Spray with spray starch, press, and carefully remove the template.

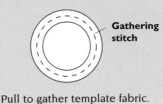

Gathering stitch

Pull to gather template fabric.

✳ FINISHING

Refer to Quilting Basics on page 91.

1. Layer the backing, batting, and quilt top; baste.

2. Quilt as desired.

3. Attach a hanging sleeve if desired.

4. Bind or finish as desired.

5. Attach a label.

Big Bear Honeymoon

9 "I think he's cute," fifteen-year-old Benni Ramsey whispered to her best friend, Elvia Aragon. English literature had halted for a moment when the new transfer student walked into the room.

Elvia glanced over at the young man who slipped into a front-row desk. She shrugged. "Not my type."

"I wasn't thinking about you." Benni gazed at the boy with the easy smile. She'd seen him three hours earlier in first-period geometry, but she'd been late, so missed him being introduced.

Benni watched him squeeze into his seat, trying to fit his tall, lanky frame into the impossibly small desks that high schools provided for students. Not difficult for barely five-footers like Benni and Elvia, but agony for students like...

"Jack," he answered the teacher with a soft Southern drawl. "Jack Harper."

Everyone turned to stare at him. New students were unusual at San Celina High School. Most kids here had known each other since kindergarten.

Jack Harper. Benni liked the sound of his name. Simple, direct, solid-sounding. Someone you could talk to, someone who would be there when they said they would, someone you'd trust your horse with.

She pulled at a strand of her long, reddish-blonde curls. Listen to me, she thought. I've got his personality all decided just because I like his name. She smiled to herself. It wasn't just his name. She also liked the way he came into the room so confidently, looking around with an open smile. Most fifteen-year-old boys were either obnoxiously cocky or so shy that their eyes seemed to be continually searching the ground for something. She also liked the simplicity of his clothes—clean white T-shirt, faded Wranglers, dark brown Ropers. His forearms were tanned a deep mahogany. He wasn't a city boy.

"Yes, ma'am," he replied to the teacher's question about whether he'd read *To Kill a Mockingbird* in his last English class in Lubbock, Texas. "We read it last semester."

Texas, Benni thought. That explains the drawl. And the "ma'am." It was how Benni was brought up, to say "ma'am" and "sir" to authority figures, because her daddy and gramma Dove were from Arkansas. But you didn't hear it much around the central coast. Adults were much more casual in California.

She cast curious glances at him throughout most of the discussion of Scout's scene with the lynch mob outside Tom Robinson's jail cell. He didn't join into the conversation, but he didn't make any smart remarks either like some of the other boys.

I'm going to say hi to him, she wrote in a note that she passed to Elvia.

Bobby will be mad, Elvia wrote back.

So? We're not going steady, Benni replied.

■ The Carnegie Library in San Luis Obispo, built in 1905, is now the San Luis County Historical Museum. Dove and her cronies often meet here to plan Historical Society functions in my fictional town of San Celina.

■ Benni buys chicken feed, hay, horse tack, dog food, and much of her Western clothing at the Farm Supply. It is truly a store for all tastes and seasons (though I doubt Elvia would shop there).

■ Strawberry fields have always been a huge part of San Luis Obispo County's history. There was a good reason why Benni's late husband Jack's favorite ice cream was strawberry!

Meet me at the flagpole when you get your lunch, Elvia wrote. *I want to hear what happened.*

When class ended, Benni lingered near her desk, the one closest to the door, pretending to look for something in her fringed leather purse. It was lunch hour so she had plenty of time.

"Hi," Jack Harper said to her as he walked by.

"Hi," she said glancing up into his warm brown eyes. Her face started to feel hot. Great, that meant she was blushing. Why did she always give her feelings away? Had he seen her sneaking peeks at him during class? That made her want to melt into a big puddle like that witch in *The Wizard of Oz.*

She continued to dig through her purse until she knew he was gone.

He probably thinks I'm an idiot, she thought. Why couldn't she have made a halfway intelligent comment about *To Kill a Mockingbird?* She'd read the book five times and knew some of the scenes by heart. Then again, maybe he would have thought that was nerdy. She sighed, gathered up her books, and started for the classroom door. Being fifteen was awful. She'd be glad when she was an adult and knew how to handle situations like this without feeling awkward.

Outside, in the almost empty hallway, Jack Harper stood waiting for her.

"Find what you were looking for?" he asked.

Benni felt her face grow warm again. "Uh, yes."

"So, what's good for lunch here?" he asked, grinning down at her.

Though her face was still red, she couldn't help smiling back. "Actually, nothing."

He threw back his head and laughed. "Then I should feel right at home. It was the same at my old school."

"In Texas?" she asked.

He nodded, reached over, and took her stack of books without asking. "We moved here two weeks ago. My dad bought the Johnston ranch."

"That's right over the hill from our ranch!"

He grinned again. "I know."

How, she wanted to ask, but didn't.

"Actually, the tri-tip sandwich isn't too gross," she said as they walked toward the cafeteria. "But not as good as what my dad makes. You and your family should come to one of our barbecues."

"I'm sure my parents would like that." He paused, then said, "So would I."

She tucked her chin into her chest and smiled. She liked this Jack Harper. There was just something about his smile.

When they reached the red brick cafeteria, he asked, "Do you have someone to eat lunch with?"

She thought of Elvia waiting by the flagpole. "Actually, I do. But how about tomorrow?"

He handed her books back to her. "Great! I'll bring you some of my mom's spice cake. It's radical."

"I love spice cake." She stood next to the entrance to the cafeteria trying to think of something else to say, something to prolong their encounter. But she was also excited about telling Elvia what just happened.

"You going to this?" Jack pointed to a poster advertising a ski trip to Big Bear Lake in the San Gabriel Mountains.

She shook her head no. "I've never skied."

"Me either," he said. "But Big Bear Lake sounds kinda cool. Like it would be a good place to go on, say, your honeymoon." He grinned at her, then turned and loped away. "See you tomorrow, Benni Louise Ramsey," he called over his shoulder.

It was few minutes before she realized that she'd never actually told him her name.

"Well?" Elvia said when Benni walked up to the flagpole.

"I think I'm in love," Benni said.

■ The barn on either the Ramsey or Harper ranches would have looked similar to this one.

Big Bear Honeymoon

Designed by Margrit Hall

Quilted by Ginny Jaranowski

Finished Block Size: 7"

Finished Quilt Size: 74" x 88"

Fabric graciously supplied by RJR Fabrics.

FABRICS AND CUTTING

Template patterns are located on the pullout.

FABRIC COLOR	FABRIC AMOUNT	CUTTING DIRECTIONS
Cream Background	$2^3/4$ yards	Cut 10 strips $7^1/2$" wide, then cut into 80 A's for blocks. Cut 1 strip $3^1/2$" wide, then cut into 16 rectangles $3^1/2$" x $1^1/2$" for corner units. Cut 1 strip $1^1/2$" wide, then cut into 16 squares $1^1/2$" x $1^1/2$" for corner units. Cut 2 strips $2^1/8$" wide, then cut into 32 squares $2^1/8$" x $2^1/8$" for corner units.
Dark Brown	$1^3/8$ yards	Cut 1 strip $6^1/8$" wide, then cut into 4 B's for blocks. Cut 6 strips $2^1/2$" wide, and set aside for 3rd border. Cut 9 strips $2^1/4$" wide for binding.
Gold	$1^1/3$ yards	Cut 4 strips $6^1/8$" wide, then cut into 20 B's for blocks. Cut 6 strips $2^1/2$" wide, and set aside for 3rd border.
Gold 2	$1^1/2$ yards	Cut 6 strips $6^1/8$" wide, then cut into 32 B's for blocks. Cut 7 strips $2^1/2$" wide, and set aside for 3rd border.
Beige	$1^3/8$ yards	Cut 4 strips $6^1/8$" wide, then cut into 20 B's for blocks. Cut 1 strip $2^1/2$" wide, then cut into 16 squares $2^1/2$" x $2^1/2$" for corner units. Cut 6 strips $2^1/2$" wide, and set aside for 3rd border.
Brown	$7/8$ yard	Cut 1 strip $6^1/8$" wide, then cut 4 B's for blocks. Cut 7 strips $2^1/2$" wide, and set aside for 3rd border.
Dark Brown 2	$3/4$ yard	Cut 2 strips $2^1/8$" wide, then cut into 32 squares $2^1/8$" x $2^1/8$" for corner units. Cut 8 strips 2" wide, and set aside for 2nd border.
Red	$3/8$ yard	Cut 1 strip $1^1/2$" wide, then cut into 4 squares $1^1/2$" x $1^1/2$" for corner units. Cut 8 strips 1" wide, and set aside for 1st border.
Backing	$5^3/8$ yards	Piece lengthwise.

■ Another view of the Carnegie Library; Benni kissed her late husband, Jack, in the garden and had a confrontation with her second husband, Gabe, in *Steps to the Altar*.

■ A typical Western barn, all practical use and homely beauty

Press seams in the direction of the arrows unless otherwise indicated.

● BLOCK ASSEMBLY

1. Refering to the quilt photo on page 21 and the diagram on page 24, arrange the blocks. Fold a background A and dark brown B in half to find the centers. Finger-press a crease at the center.

2. Place A and B right sides together, with B (convex curve) on the bottom and A (concave curve) on top. Match the centers and pin, then match and pin the outer edges. Continue to pin across the seam, clipping the concave curve as necessary to ease across the convex curve. Sew carefully. Open and press.

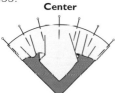

Center

Pin and sew carefully.

Open and press.

3. Sew a B of each fabric to a background A to make the number of blocks listed below.

Dark Brown: 4 blocks
Gold: 20 blocks
Gold 2: 32 blocks
Beige: 20 blocks
Brown: 4 blocks

● QUILT ASSEMBLY

1. Refering to the quilt photo on page 21 and the diagram on page 24, arrange the blocks. Sew the blocks together in rows. Press seams in alternating directions.

2. Sew the rows together and press.

First Border

Before cutting all final borders, measure your quilt top to confirm measurements for the strip lengths.

1. Sew the red 1"-wide strips together end-to-end in pairs, and cut 2 of the long strips to measure 56½" long. Sew to the top and bottom of the quilt and press.

2. Cut the remaining long red strips to measure 71½" long, and sew to the sides of the quilt. Press.

Second Border

1. Sew dark brown 2"-wide strips together end-to-end in pairs, and cut 2 of the long strips to measure 57½" long. Sew to the top and bottom of the quilt. Press.

2. Cut the remaining long dark brown strips to measure 74½" long, and sew to the sides of the quilt. Press.

Bear Paw Corner Unit Assembly

1. Draw a diagonal line across the wrong side of the 32 cream 2⅛" x 2⅛" background squares.

2. Place the marked background squares right sides together with 2⅛" dark brown squares and sew ¼" away from each side of the marked diagonal line.

Make 32.

3. Cut in half on the diagonal line. Press seams open and square up to 1½" x 1½" square. Make 64 half-square triangle units.

Half-square triangle unit Make 64.

4. Sew 2 half-square triangle units together, arranging brown triangles as shown to make Unit A. Press seams open. Make 16.

Unit A Make 16.

5. Sew remaining half-square triangle units together, arranging brown triangles as shown to make Unit B. Press seams open. Make 16.

Unit B Make 16.

6. Sew a 1½" background square to the right side of Unit A to make Unit C. Press. Make 16.

Unit C Make 16.

7. Sew a Unit B to the top of a 2¹/₂" beige square. Press. Sew a Unit C to the left side of the 2¹/₂" square to make Unit D. Press.

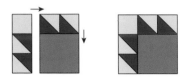

Unit D Make 16.

8. Sew Unit D's to both sides of a 1¹/₂" x 3¹/₂" cream background rectangle to make Section 1. Press. Make 8.

9. Sew 1¹/₂" x 3¹/₂" background rectangles to 2 opposite sides of a 1¹/₂" x 1¹/₂" red square to make Section 2. Press.

10. Sew Section 1's to both sides of Section 2. Press. Make 4 Bear Paw corner units.

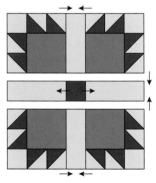

Bear Paw corner unit Make 4.

Third Border

1. Sew the 2¹/₂"-wide strips of beige, dark brown, gold, gold 2, and brown together to make Strip Set 1. Press. Make 6 strip sets and cut into 26 segments 7¹/₂" wide.

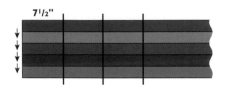

Strip Set 1 Make 6 and cut into 26 segments.

2. Sew the 2¹/₂"-wide strips of gold 2 and brown together to make Strip Set 2. Press and cut into 2 segments 7¹/₂" wide.

3. Sew 6 Strip Set 1 segments together for the top and bottom borders. Press. Make 2, and sew to the top and bottom of the quilt. Press.

4. Sew 7 Strip Set 1 segments together for the side borders, and add 1 Strip Set 2 segment. Press. Make 2. Sew a Bear Paw corner unit to each end of the side borders and press. Sew to the sides of the quilt and press.

◉ FINISHING

Refer to Quilting Basics on page 91.

1. Layer the backing, batting, and quilt top; baste.

2. Quilt as desired.

3. Attach a hanging sleeve if desired.

4. Bind or finish as desired.

5. Attach a label.

Quilt Assembly Diagram

Family Chain

by Benni Ramsey
History 102—Oral History assignment
San Celina Union High School
May 15, 1974

9 was born in 1958 in Sugartree, Arkansas, but I mostly consider California my home because I have been here since I was two years old. It was 1960 when my parents decided to leave Arkansas, where they had lived their whole lives, and move to the Central Coast of California. They bought a 500 acre-ranch with money they got from some insurance. My dad visited a friend here once and said he'd always remembered how beautiful it was. Daddy calls it a "bovine paradise." I don't remember the train ride out here, though my father says I cried almost the entire way. My mother died when I was six, so I can't ask her what she remembered.

My earliest memory of California was when I fell off a wooden fence that surrounds our corral next to the barn. My dad said that happened when I was four. Somehow I got away from my mother and wandered out the back door to the corral where I climbed the fence. Apparently I was sitting on the fence just fine, watching the horses, until my mother looked out the kitchen window and saw me. She screamed my name, which scared me, causing me to pitch forward. The only thing I remember is the sound of air rushing past my ears and the dark ground rising up to meet me. I don't remember being afraid, more like surprised.

My next earliest memory was sitting on a horse and kicking my feet against his sides trying to get him to move. I remember feeling frustrated because he just stood there, and I remember laughter in the background, though I don't recall who was laughing. My dad doesn't remember this incident, so I'm assuming it must have happened with my mother. I don't really remember the first time I was ever on a horse, though that might have been it. I don't remember ever <u>not</u> riding horses.

My dad's father, Jacob Luke Ramsey, was a farmer near Sugartree, Arkansas. He grew tobacco and cotton and a big vegetable garden. They had hogs and chickens and a milk cow. My dad said he was five when he learned how to milk a cow. Daddy is the oldest of six children and was expected to help out around the farm. His brothers and sisters are named Kate, Ruth, Luke, Clarence, and Arnie. My uncle Arnie is only six years older than me. My grampa, Jake Ramsey, died when I was five years old. I only saw him once when he

■ There is nothing cuter and more frustrating than a baby calf!

■ I based the Frio Saloon in *Dove in the Window* on this place. It's a favorite hangout for many San Luis Obispo County folks.

and my gramma Dove drove out to California to see our new ranch. I remember he smelled like something spicy, it burnt my nose. My dad told me later it was his bay rum aftershave. Grampa taught me how to sing "Row, row, row your boat." According to my parents I drove them crazy for months after he left because I wouldn't stop singing it. My gramma Dove said he had a beautiful voice, that he often sang solos in Sugartree Baptist Church. He died from a heart attack out in the field when he was working. He was in the middle of singing a song when he died. Gramma Dove had my uncle ride bareback to the nearest neighbor a half-mile away where they had a phone. She said she sat with grampa for the whole hour it took for the doctor to arrive. She said she was always glad for that time alone with him, before the funeral home people took him away. She told him all the things she wished she'd told him their whole life. She told me to remember this one thing if I don't ever listen to anything else: Don't forget to tell the people you love all the things in your heart. You never know when the hourglass sand is going to run out.

My gramma Dove is called Dove by everyone, even her kids and grandkids. My dad is the one who started it. Since grampa always called her that, it ended up being the first word my dad learned. It just took, as Dove would say, and no one calls her anything else. She has called me honeybun for as long as I can remember. She doesn't call anyone else that except me. She calls all her other grandchildren (she has twelve at last count) sweetie or punkin. I don't know if that makes me special, having a different nickname, but I think I might be her favorite even though she'd probably smack me upside the head for bragging. She claims she loves all her grandkids equally, and I think she does, but I'm sort of a halfway grandchild, halfway child for her because she's raised me since I was six. She left everything in Arkansas to come out to take care of me when my own mother died. Dove was forty-six years old and my uncle Arnie, who was twelve, was her only child left at home so he came too. That's why he feels more like my brother than my uncle. He used to tease me a lot when I was a kid and followed him around everywhere. He nicknamed me "Piglet" which always made me mad because, actually, I'm a very neat person, most of the time. He is the big slob. He's twenty-two now and we get along a little better, though not much. Daddy says that Dove spoiled Arnie too much and that is why he is good for nothing except decorating a horse. My dad really does like his youngest brother even if Arnie is, as Daddy would say, wild as a corncrib rat. Dove says they both should use their eyes a little more and their mouths a little less.

Daddy met my mama when she was seventeen and working as a waitress at a coffeeshop in Sugartree. But this report is only supposed to be a thousand words so I guess that's another story.

■ The hills seem to go on forever.

Family Chain

Designed by Margrit Hall
Made by Rhoda Nelson
Quilted by Ginny Jaranowski

Finished Block Size: $10\frac{1}{2}$"
Finished Quilt Size: $67\frac{1}{2}$" x $88\frac{1}{2}$"
Fabric graciously supplied by Hoffman California Fabrics.

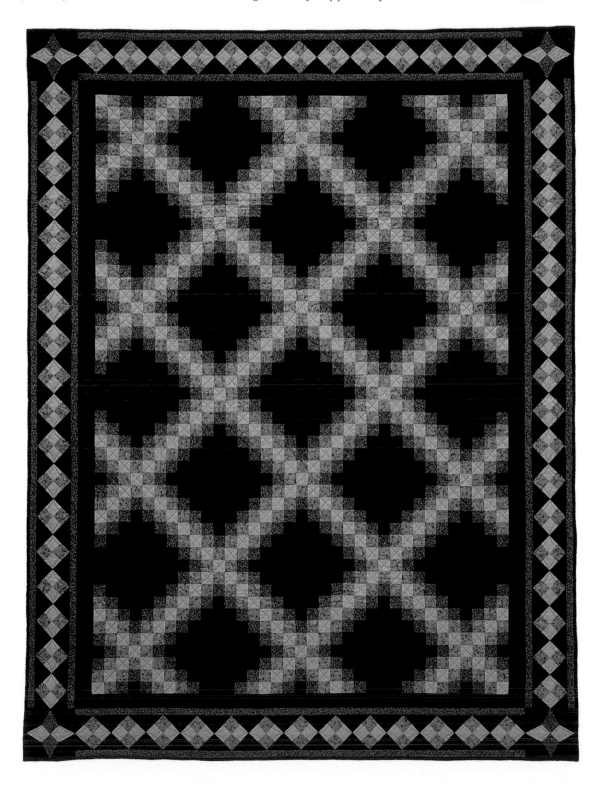

◆ FABRICS AND CUTTING

Template patterns are located on page 31.

FABRIC COLOR	FABRIC AMOUNT	CUTTING DIRECTIONS
Black	4 yards	Cut 4 strips 2" wide for Block A. Cut 4 strips 5" wide for Block B. Cut 4 strips 8" wide, then cut into 17 squares 8" x 8" for Block B. Cut 4 strips $1^7/_8$" wide for side 1st borders. Cut 4 strips 2" wide for top and bottom 1st borders. Cut 2 strips $3^5/_8$" wide, then cut into 16 B's for 2nd border star corner block. Cut 1 strip 3" wide. Cut into 8 squares 3" x 3", then cut each square once on the diagonal to make 16 D triangles for 2nd border. Cut 5 strips $5^1/_2$" wide. Cut into 29 squares $5^1/_2$" x $5^1/_2$", then cut each square twice on the diagonal to make 116 C triangles for 2nd border. Cut 9 strips $2^1/_4$" wide for binding.
Light Green	$1^3/_8$ yards	Cut 20 strips 2" wide for Block A and 2nd border. Cut 1 strip $3^5/_8$" wide, then cut into 8 A's for 2nd border star corner block.
Medium Green	2 yards	Cut 31 strips 2" wide for Block A, Block B, and 2nd border.
Dark Green	$2^1/_8$ yards	Cut 20 strips 2" wide for Block A and Block B. Cut 1 strip $3^5/_8$" wide, then cut into 8 A's for 2nd border star corner block. Cut 16 strips $1^3/_8$" wide for 2nd border.
Backing	$5^3/_8$ yards	Piece lengthwise.

Press seams in the direction of the arrows, unless otherwise indicated.

◆ BLOCK A ASSEMBLY

1. Sew together 2"-wide strips of black, light green, medium green, and dark green to make Groups 1–4 as shown. Press. Cut into 2"-wide segments.

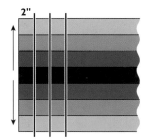

Group 1 Make 2 strip sets.
Cut 36 segments.

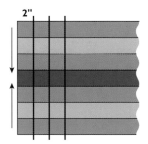

Group 2 Make 2 strip sets.
Cut 36 segments.

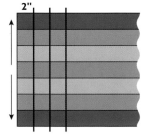

Group 3 Make 2 strip sets.
Cut 36 segments.

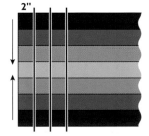

Group 4 Make 1 strip set.
Cut 18 segments.

2. Sew Groups 1–4 segments together to make Block A. Make 18.

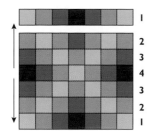

Block A Make 18.

BLOCK B ASSEMBLY

1. Sew together 2"-wide strips of medium green and dark green with 5"-wide strips of black to make Groups 5 and 6 as shown. Press. Cut into 2" segments.

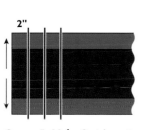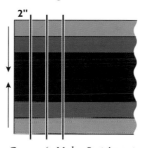

Group 5 Make 2 strip sets.
Cut 34 segments

Group 6 Make 2 strip sets.
Cut 34 segments.

2. Sew Group 5 segments to the top and bottom of a black 8" x 8" square. Press.

3. Sew Group 6 segments to each side to make Block B. Press. Make 17.

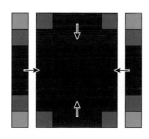

Block B Make 17.

QUILT ASSEMBLY

1. Alternate Blocks A and B, and sew together in rows. Press toward Block B.

2. Sew the rows together, and press seams open to form the quilt center.

First Border

Before cutting all final borders, measure your quilt top to confirm measurements for the strip lengths.

1. Sew black $1^7/_8$" strips together end-to-end in pairs. Cut 2 strips 53" long. Sew to the top and bottom of the quilt. Press.

2. Sew black 2" strips together end-to-end in pairs. Cut 2 strips 77" long. Sew to the sides of the quilt. Press.

Star Corner Block Assembly

1. Mark dots on A pieces and sew a light green A to a dark green A to make Unit A. Sew to the dot and backstitch. Sew just to the dot; do not sew through the dot. Press seam open. Make 8.

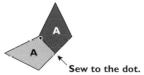

Unit A Make 8.

2. Sew 2 Unit A's together to make the star. Sew between the dots, backstitching at each end. Press seams open.

3. Set in a black B at each corner of Unit A. Sew to the dot and backstitch. Sew seam 1, then seam 2. Press toward Unit A. Make 4.

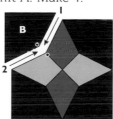

Make 4.

Second Border

1. Sew a 2"-wide light green strip and a 2"-wide medium green strip together. Press. Make 7 strip sets and cut into 124 segments 2" wide.

Make 7 strip sets. Cut into 124 segments.

2. Sew 2 segments together to make a four-patch unit. Press. Make 62 four-patch units.

Make 62.

3. Sew black C triangles to opposite sides of a four-patch unit to make Unit 1. Make sure the medium green units are at the top and bottom and the light green units are on each side. Press. Make 54.

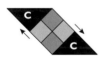

Unit 1 Make 54.

4. Sew 1 black C triangle and 2 black D triangles to 3 sides of 8 four-patch units to make Unit 2. Press. Make 8.

Unit 2 Make 8.

5. For the top and bottom 2nd border, sew 11 Unit 1's together. Sew a Unit 2 to each end. Press seams open.

6. For each of the side 2nd borders, sew 16 Unit 1's together. Sew a Unit 2 to each end. Press seams open.

Make 2 for top and bottom and 2 for the side borders.

7. Piece dark green 1³⁄₈"-wide strips together end-to-end as needed, and cut 2 strips approximately 80" long and 2 strips approximately 60" long.

8. Sew 60"-long dark green strips to the top and bottom of each top-and-bottom-pieced border unit. Trim even with the ends of the pieced border unit. Press toward the border strips.

9. Sew 80"-long dark green strips to the top and bottom of each of the side-pieced border units. Trim even with the ends of the pieced border unit. Press toward the border strips.

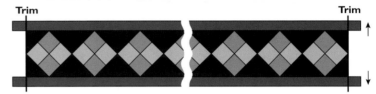

10. Sew the pieced top and bottom borders to the top and bottom of the quilt. Press.

11. Sew a star corner block to each end of the pieced side borders. Press. Sew to the sides of the quilt. Press.

FINISHING

Refer to Quilting Basics on page 91.

1. Layer the backing, batting, and quilt top; baste.

2. Quilt as desired.

3. Attach a hanging sleeve if desired.

4. Bind or finish as desired.

5. Attach a label.

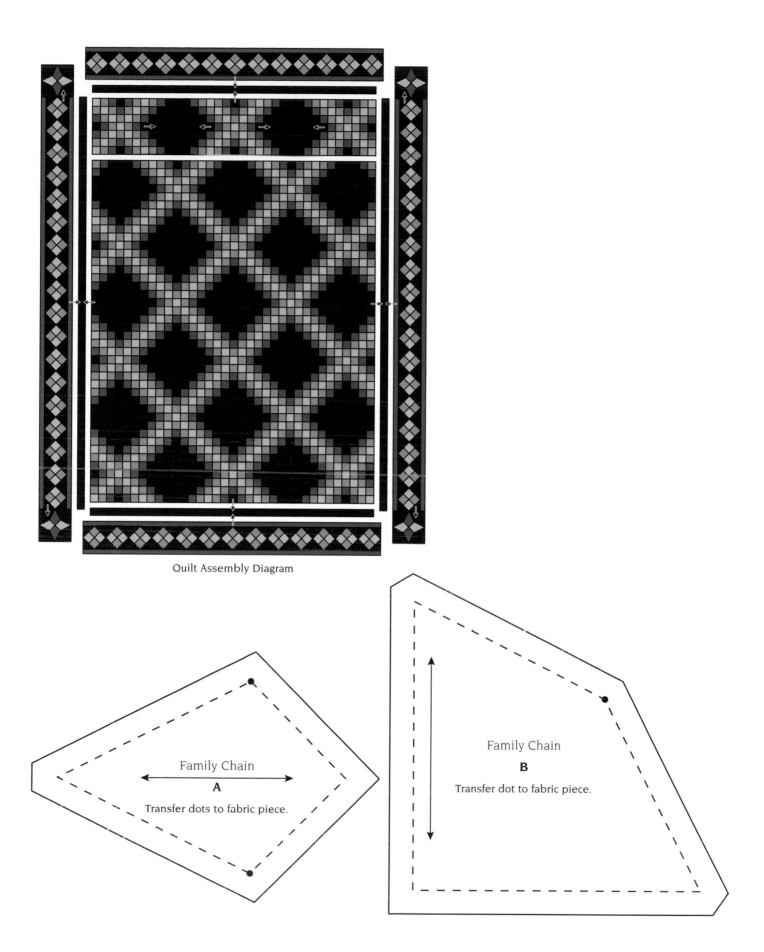

Quilt Assembly Diagram

Family Chain

A

Transfer dots to fabric piece.

Family Chain

B

Transfer dot to fabric piece.

Señor Azure

What's wrong, *mijo*?" Rogelio Ortiz asked his five-year-old son, Gabriel. His son, a handsome boy with eyes the color of the Pacific Ocean, looked ready to cry. He wouldn't, something that often worried Rogelio. Although his Mexican heritage was apparent in his smooth brown skin and thick black hair, his son was emotionally like his proud Kansas mother. Emotions ran deep but silent in Gabe's paleskinned, Kansas *madre*.

"They laughed at me in school again," Gabe said. "They said my skin is brown 'cause I drink chocolate milk. They say I'm different." Gabe looked up at his father, his blue-gray eyes angry. "I *am* different."

"*Mijo*," Rogelio said, his heart swelling with sadness, wishing he could make the hurt disappear. "Do not listen to the *niños*. They are *ignorante*." He pulled his son into his lap. "Let me tell you a story about a . . . a blue *tortuga*. His name is *Señor* Azure."

Gabe's expression became puzzled. "Azure?"

"That is a kind of blue."

"Turtles aren't blue," Gabe said, smiling now. "They're green! I've seen them at grandpa's farm."

"Not *this* turtle. He was a special *tortuga*."

His son snuggled deeper into his father's arms. "Why?"

"In a little Mexican town called Anzuelo where I was a boy there lived many *tortugas*. They gathered every day in the center of the town around the fountain to talk about their *logros*.'"

"What?"

"Their accomplishments. What they do well. Like how you gather *Abuelita* Smith's eggs without breaking them."

Gabe's face grew serious. "I broke one once, but it was an accident."

"Yes, but you try very hard to do your best and that is the most *importante*. These turtles grew up together and every day they would meet at the fountain. While they played and talked, other animals would watch and listen."

"What other animals?"

"In the fountain was a pink *pescado*, next to the mission was a brown *caballo*, standing under the palm tree was a red *zorro*, and sitting high in the tree was a *papagayo* whose feathers were the colors of the rainbow."

"I know these!" Gabe counted off the animals on his fingers. "A pink fish, a brown horse, a red fox, and a parrot!"

"Very good." He looked down at his son's beaming face, feeling like his heart would burst from love.

"What games did the *tortugas* play?"

"They would play tic-tac-toe using clam shells and tug-of-war with seaweed. They would try to play leap frog, but that is a very hard game for turtles to play. They would sing songs about the things turtles love, like the beautiful blue ocean and the warm yellow sunshine and the colorful fruit they eat. One day their life changed."

"How?"

"A new turtle moved into Anzuelo, and he wasn't like them. You see, every one of the *tortugas* was green. They were each a little different green and they each had different color markings on their shells, but they were all green. Green was the only color they'd ever seen in a turtle, so this new turtle scared them because he was blue."

"*Señor* Azure!" Gabe cried out.

"Si. He was from far, far away where turtles were blue and dogs

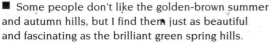
■ Some people don't like the golden-brown summer and autumn hills, but I find them just as beautiful and fascinating as the brilliant green spring hills.

were orange and cats were as purple as plums. The first time the green turtles saw him, they laughed and pointed at his plain blue shell."

"His *azure* shell."

His father nodded. "They said it was ugly and different. They would tell him to go find other blue turtles to play with. But he couldn't because there were no other blue turtles in Anzuela. When he would come home, his papa would ask him if he had fun in the town square, and he would tell him that he had great fun playing with his new friends, the green turtles."

"He lied to his papa!" Gabe said, his young face shocked.

"*Si, mijo*, but he didn't do it to be bad. He didn't want his papa to be sad because of what the other turtles said." He shifted his son's weight across his lap. "One day when Señor Azure was watching the other turtles, the *papagayo* who sat in the tree called out to him.

'Señor Azure,' the parrot called. 'I heard you came from far, far away.'

'Yes, it is many miles away across a big desert where there were snakes and coyotes and prickly cactus.'

'I've heard all the turtles are blue in this faraway place.'

'That is what my papa tells me. I do not remember much about the far-away place.'

'I have heard about this place from the seagulls. They tell me the turtles there are special.'

'No, I think they are just blue. Like me.'

'You should ask *tu padre* about it,' the parrot said, a wise look in his bright yellow eyes.

So when *Señor* Azure went home that night, he asked his papa, 'The *papagayo* says that blue turtles are special. I don't think we are. I think we are ugly. That is what the green turtles always say.' He looked down at his blue feet, ashamed that he said the thing to his papa that he'd been trying to hide.

■ The reason Gabe felt so comfortable in San Celina is that some of the country looked like Kansas.

A soft look came in his papa's eyes. 'Yes, we are different, but it is a very special difference, and you must never hold it over others when they cannot do what we can do.'

'What can we do that is special?' *Señor* Azure asked.

Then his father showed him. When a blue turtle holds his legs out in a special way, he can fly.

'Look, look!' *Señor* Azure said as he flew up into the palm trees. 'I am like the *papagayo*! I can fly!'

The next day at the square, he waited until all the green turtles arrived, and then he spread his legs and flew above their heads.

'How do you do that?' cried the green turtles. 'Can you teach us?'

But, of course, he couldn't, because you had to be a blue turtle to fly. But he could give them rides, which he did all afternoon. And even when he wasn't flying, they discovered that he was just like them in many ways. They taught him all the green turtle games, and he taught them some blue turtle games. They laughed and laughed, and no one mentioned his blue shell again."

"So," Rogelio said, "being different is always hard, but it is not always bad. Sometimes, like Señor Azure, you can use how you are different to show others how much the same we all are."

Gabe studied his father with solemn eyes. "That was a good story," he finally declared. "I wish I was blue."

Rogelio just hugged his son and laughed.

■ This angel monument is in the Catholic cemetery off Higuera Street. It is the model used for the cover of *Steps to the Altar.*

Señor Azure

Designed by Margrit Hall

Made by Rhoda Nelson

Quilted by Phyllis Reddish

Finished Quilt Size: 48¹/₂" x 39¹/₂"

Fabric graciously supplied by Timeless Treasures Fabrics.

FABRICS AND CUTTING

Patterns are located on the pullout.

FABRIC COLOR	FABRIC AMOUNT	CUTTING DIRECTIONS
Black	$1/4$ yard	Cut 4 strips 1" wide for 1st border.
Multicolor	$1^1/8$ yards	Cut 4 strips $5^1/4$" wide for 2nd border.
		Cut 5 strips $2^1/4$" wide for binding.
Light Blue	$3/8$ yard	Cut 1 strip $10^1/2$" x $38^1/2$" for sky.
Light Brown & Green	$5/8$ yard	Cut 1 strip $19^1/2$" x $38^1/2$" for ground.
Medium Brown	$1/2$ yard	Cut 1 strip $13^3/4$" wide for the mission.
Dark Brown	$1/4$ yard	Cut 1 each of RR, SS, TT, UU, VV, WW, XX, YY, ZZ, and AAA for mission doors, windows, and log ends.
Brown Gold	$1/8$ yard ($5/8$ yard if cut vertically)	Cut 1 each of NN and PP for palm tree trunks.
Medium Green	$1/4$ yard	Cut 1 each of OO and QQ for palm tree leaves.
Dark Apricot	$1/4$ yard	Cut 1 each of BBB, DDD, FFF, GGG, and JJJ for fountain.
Light Apricot	$1/4$ yard	Cut 1 each of EEE and III for fountain.
Blue Green	$1/4$ yard	Cut 1 each of CCC and HHH for water in fountain.
Lime Green	4" x 6" scrap	Cut 1 II, 2 each of JJ and KK, and 3 LL for cactus.
Brown	$2^1/2$" x $2^1/2$" scrap	Cut 1 MM for cactus flowerpot.
	6" x 7" scrap	Cut 1 GG for horse body.
Tan	6" x 6" scrap	Cut 1 each of EE and FF for horse mane and tail.
Solid Brown	$2^1/2$" x $2^1/2$" scrap	Cut 1 each of CC and DD for horse ears. Cut 4 HH for hooves.
Blue & Green Print	$2^1/2$" x $3^1/2$" scrap	Cut 1 E for parrot body.
Red & Yellow Print	5" x 5" scrap	Cut 1 C, 1 D, and 3 A for parrot wings and tail.
Gold	2" x 2" scrap	Cut 1 each of B and F for parrot beak and feet.
Pink Print	2" x $2^1/2$" scrap	Cut 1 V for fish body.
Solid Pink	2" x 2" scrap	Cut 1 each of T, U, and W for fish fins.
Red	$3^1/2$" x 15" scrap	Cut 1 each of X, Y, Z, AA, and BB for fox.
Medium Blue	$3^1/2$" x 6" scrap	Cut 1 each of Q and R for blue turtle body.
Dark Blue	$3^1/2$" x $3^1/2$" scrap	Cut 1 S for blue turtle shell.
Light Green	$1/8$ yard or 6 scrap pieces 3" x 3" each	Cut 1 G and 1 G reverse, 1 N, and 2 O's and 1 O reverse for green turtle backs.
Dark Green	$1/8$ yard or 7 scrap pieces 3" x 3" each	Cut 1 each of H and H reverse; 1 each of I and I reverse; 1 each of J, K, L, and M; and 2 P and 1 P reverse for green turtle bodies.
Green	$3/8$" x 4" strip	For seaweed between turtles
Blue Glitter Netting (optional)	$1/4$ yard	Cut 1 each of CCC and HHH for water.
Backing	$2^1/2$ yards	Piece vertically.
Paper-Backed Fusible Webbing	$2^1/2$ yards	

Other materials: thread for buttonhole stitch

Press seams in the direction of the arrows, unless otherwise indicated.

QUILT BASE

See Quilting Basics on page 92 for information about fusible appliqué.

1. Sew the 10^1/$_2$" x 38^1/$_2$" piece of sky fabric to the 19^1/$_2$" x 38^1/$_2$" piece of ground fabric. Press seam open.

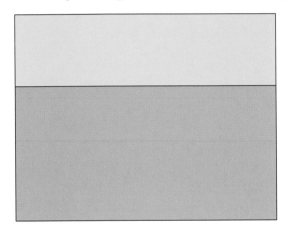

2. Fuse paper-backed fusible web to the back of the 13^1/$_2$" x 38^1/$_2$" piece of mission fabric. Cut the fused fabric at an angle from the top-left corner to 7^1/$_2$" up from the bottom of the right side.

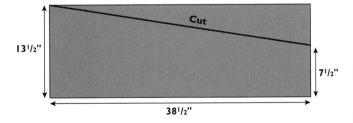

3. Place a mark 6^3/$_4$" up from the bottom-left corner of the mission and 2^1/$_2$" up from the bottom-right corner of the mission. Use a pencil to draw a line between the marks for placement of the doors and windows.

4. Draw another line 2^1/$_2$" down from the top of the mission for placement of the logs.

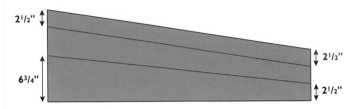

5. Fuse the mission 13" up from the bottom edge of the ground/sky unit. Option: Fuse doors, windows, and logs in place before fusing mission to the ground/sky unit. See Hint on following page.

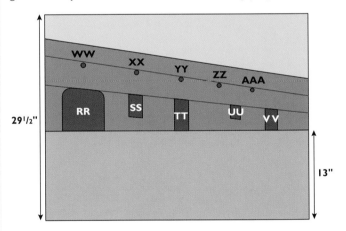

⊞ APPLIQUÉ

> ### Hint
>
> Using an appliqué pressing sheet, fuse the components of the mission, animals, small palm tree, fountain, and cactus together, then place and fuse to the quilt.

1. Trace the patterns A–III on the paper side of the fusible web. (For reverse shapes, lay the templates face down.) Cut around the patterns, leaving at least $1/4$" around the designs. Fuse to the back of the fabric, and cut out the patterns on the line.

2. Using the photo and diagram as a guide, lay out the doors (RR, TT, and VV), the windows (SS and UU), and the logs (WW, XX, YY, ZZ, and AAA) on the mission and fuse. Fuse all the remaining appliqués except the large palm leaves (OO) and bird (A, B, C, D, E, and F) to the body of the quilt. Sew a buttonhole stitch around each appliqué piece.

⊞ QUILT ASSEMBLY

First Border

Before cutting all final borders, measure your quilt top to confirm measurements for the strip lengths.

1. Cut 2 of the 1"-wide black strips to measure $38^{1}/_{2}$" long. Sew to the top and bottom of the quilt, and press toward the border.

2. Cut remaining 2 strips to measure $30^{1}/_{2}$" long. Sew to the sides of the quilt, and press toward the border.

Second Border

1. Cut 2 of the multicolor $5^{1}/_{4}$"-wide strips to measure $39^{1}/_{2}$" long. Sew to the top and bottom of the quilt, and press toward the 2nd border.

2. Cut remaining 2 strips to measure 40" long. Sew to the sides of the quilt, and press toward the 2nd border.

3. Fuse large palm leaves and bird to the quilt. Sew a buttonhole stitch around the palm leaves and bird.

4. Use a permanent marker to fill in details on the animals (eyes, mouths, etc.).

Embellishments

NETTING ON WATER (OPTIONAL)

1. Place blue netting CCC and HHH over water in the fountain. (The netting in the quilt had glitter on it.)

2. Machine stitch around the edge of the netting with matching thread.

3. Using blue metallic thread, hand sew larger random stitches over the surface of the water.

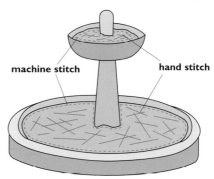

machine stitch   hand stitch

SEAWEED

1. Cut sawtooth edges along both long sides of the $3/8$" x 4" dark green strip.

2. Place on quilt between the turtles. Stitch along the center of the strip to attach it to the background.

⊞ FINISHING

Refer to Quilting Basics on page 91.

1. Layer the backing, batting, and quilt top; baste.

2. Quilt as desired.

3. Attach a hanging sleeve if desired.

4. Bind or finish as desired.

5. Attach a label.

Kansas Troubles

"You did what?" said Gabe's mother, Kathryn. Her Midwestern accent flattened on the last word.

"I got married," Gabe answered, glancing over at the bedroom. His new bride, Benni, hadn't gotten up yet. They'd been home from Las Vegas for two days, and he'd put off calling his mother as long as he could. It wasn't that he was afraid, exactly. No, scratch that. He was afraid. A forty-three-year-old ex-Marine, ex-undercover cop, current chief of police of a good-sized college town, and he was afraid of his mother.

"Like any intelligent, normal man would be," his captain, Jim Cleary, had said with a laugh when Gabe mentioned he was nervous about telling his mother about his spur-of-the-moment marriage.

"To whom?" she asked, her voice cool as the Arkansas River she lived next to in Derby, Kansas.

"I told you I was dating someone . . . Benni Harper. A woman here in San Celina. She was a history major." He didn't know why he threw that last piece of information in there, except that his mother, a fifth-grade teacher, respected education.

"The woman you've only known three months?" she said. Her question said everything she was thinking. His mother was like that, few words with lots of complex meanings. So unlike his Mexican father, who had died when Gabe was sixteen. Rogelio Ortiz loved to talk and loved people. If he'd been alive, Gabe would have called him and asked him to tell Kathryn the news.

"You'll love her, Mom," he said, running his hand through his black hair, keeping an eye on the closed bedroom door. He didn't want Benni to hear this phone call. He was afraid she would see the hesitation on his face and assume that he hadn't been sure about marrying her. He'd actually never been more sure of anything in his life. "We're going to try to come to Kansas. Maybe in the next few months, if I can manage some time off."

"Who exactly is this woman you married?" she asked.

He sat down on the sofa, switched the phone to the other ear, trying to buy time. His mother's even breathing was so quiet it sounded like she'd hung up.

He took a deep breath. "She's great, Mom. She's lived here in San Celina most of her life. She works as a curator to a folk art museum. Her family owns a cattle ranch."

"Kids?" Kathryn asked.

He knew what she was really asking. Had he married a divorcé? She was pretty judgmental about that, which was funny considering both he and one of his twin sisters were divorced.

"No. She's a widow."

"How *old* is this woman?"

"Thirty-four."

"Oh." He heard her voice soften slightly. "That's . . . very tragic."

"He was her childhood sweetheart. He died in an auto accident."

"What does she look like?"

Another veiled question. His mother was Anglo, his father Hispanic, and his first wife, Lydia, had been Hispanic. She was also very beautiful. He wasn't sure if his mother was asking if Benni was as beautiful as his first wife or if she were white.

"I think she's gorgeous," he said. "Reddish-blonde hair, incredible hazel eyes, about five-foot-one. She rode before she could walk."

■ Cemeteries inspire me as a writer. When I travel, I like to see the local cemeteries, especially the older ones.

"That's nice," his mother said.

Wrong thing to say, he thought. That's not something that would impress his mother. Maybe he should move back to Benni's education. "She loves to read. Always has a book with her no matter where she goes."

"Ummm," Kathryn said.

He wanted to bellow like a bull. He loved his mother deeply, but she was so hard to understand. Not for the first time, he tried to imagine how in the world his taciturn mother and gregarious father ended up happily married.

"Well," Kathryn said. "If you love her . . ."

"I do, Mom. More than any woman I've ever known."

She was quiet for a moment. This was something he'd never said before. Not even with Lydia, whom he'd married because she was pregnant with their son, Sam.

"Then I'm sure she must be a nice girl," she said, though her voice said she doubted it. Gabe was her oldest child and her only son. If he knew she thought, no woman would ever be good enough.

The bedroom door opened, and Benni walked out. Her curly hair was in a sexy tangle, and she was wearing one of his navy blue San Celina Police Department T-shirts. She gave him a sleepy smile and wandered into the kitchen, looking for coffee. He gazed at her strong, slender legs and felt desire start to stir in the pit of his stomach.

"Gabe?" His mother's voice brought him back from the sensual thoughts clouding his brain.

"Yes, Mom, I'm here."

"I just hope you know what you're doing."

"I do." The words reminded him of their wedding ceremony in Las Vegas.

"See you soon. I miss you."

"I miss you too. Hug the sisters for me."

By the time Benni came into the living room, holding a steaming cup of coffee, he was off the phone.

"Who was that?" she asked, sitting down beside him.

"My mom."

Her nose wrinkled, then she took a sip of her coffee. Her hazel eyes smiled at him over the rim.

"She says she can't wait to meet you," he lied.

She threw back her head and laughed. The delicate hollow on her neck, right below her throat, caused desire to dart through his veins like mercury. He already knew that when he kissed her there, she was his.

"Right," she said, looking at him, her face amused. "Don't forget, Friday. I've been married before. She probably gave you the third degree and has already decided I'm not good enough for her baby boy."

He stared at her, amazed. How did women know these things?

She set the coffee down and took his hand in hers. "Hey, she's a mom. It's her job to be suspicious. Remember how my gramma Dove was with you until she knew your true intentions. Give me some time. I'll win her over."

"How much time do you think it'll take?" he asked, not certain she really understood what his mother was like.

She grinned at him and kissed his palm. "Oh, about thirty or forty years."

■ A windmill that reminds us of SLO's rural past.

■ In *Kansas Troubles*, much of the plot revolves around the Amish. There is a community of them near the town of Yoder, which I call Miller in the book.

Kansas Troubles

Designed by Margrit Hall
Made by Cathryn Tallman-Evans
Appliquéd and quilted by Kelly Gallagher-Abbott

Finished Block Size: 10"
Finished Quilt Size: 41" x 41"
Fabric graciously supplied by Hoffman California Fabrics.

⬛ FABRICS AND CUTTING

Template patterns are located on the pullout.

FABRIC COLOR	FABRIC AMOUNT	CUTTING DIRECTIONS
Light Green Print	³/₈ yard	Cut 3 strips 3" wide.
Yellow Print	³/₈ yard	Cut 1 strip 3" wide. Cut 1 strip 3¹/₂" wide. Cut 1 strip 2³/₄" wide.
Brown	¹/₂ yard	Cut 1 strip 5¹/₂" wide, then cut into 9 rectangles 5¹/₂" x 3". Cut 2 strips 3" wide.
Gold	¹/₄ yard	Cut 1 strip 5¹/₂" wide, then cut 9 A's.
Dark Green Print	³/₈ yard	Cut 1 strip 2¹/₂" wide. Cut 1 strip 5¹/₂" wide, then cut into 9 B's.
Orange Print	⁵/₈ yard	Cut 2 strips 3¹/₄" wide. Cut 5 strips 2¹/₄" wide for binding.
Green with Orange Small Print	¹/₄ yard	Cut 1 strip 2³/₄" wide.
Dark Green Solid	¹/₄ yard	Cut 4 strips 1¹/₂" wide for 1st border.
Cream	¹/₄ yard	Cut 2 strips 2¹/₈" wide, then cut into 24 squares 2¹/₈" x 2¹/₈" for corner units. Cut 1 strip 1⁵/₈" wide, then cut into 12 squares 1⁵/₈" x 1⁵/₈" for corner units.
Orange	¹/₄ yard	Cut 2 strips 2¹/₈" wide, then cut into 24 squares 2¹/₈" x 2¹/₈" for corner units. Cut 1 strip 2" wide. Cut into 12 squares 2" x 2", then cut each square once on the diagonal to make 24 triangles for corner units.
Yellow & Orange	¹/₄ yard	Cut 1 strip 3¹/₈" wide. Cut into 6 squares 3¹/₈" x 3¹/₈", then cut each square once on the diagonal to make 12 triangles for corner units.
Medium Olive	³/₄ yard	Cut 1 strip 5³/₈" wide. Cut into 6 squares 5³/₈" x 5³/₈", then cut each square once on the diagonal to make 12 triangles for corner units. Set remainder aside for leaf and cornhusk appliqué pieces.
Orange & Green Large Print	³/₄ yard	Cut 4 strips 5" wide for 2nd border.
Light Green Solid	¹/₂ yard	Set aside for leaf and cornhusk appliqué pieces.
Medium Dark Green	¹/₂ yard	Set aside for leaf, cornhusk, and cornstalk appliqué pieces.
Yellow Solid	¹/₄ yard	Set aside for corn and tassel appliqué pieces.
Backing	2⁵/₈ yards	Piece together.
Paper-Backed Fusible Webbing	2³/₄ yards	

Other materials: appliqué pressing sheet, thread for buttonhole stitch

Press seams in the direction of the arrows, unless otherwise indicated.

BLOCK ASSEMBLY

1. Sew a 3"-wide strip of light green print to a 3"-wide strip of yellow print to make Unit A. Press and cut into 9 segments 3" wide.

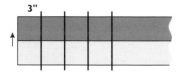

3"

Cut 9 segments for Unit A.

2. Sew a 5¹/₂" x 3" brown rectangle to the right side of each Unit A and press to make Section 1. Make 9.

Section 1 Make 9.

3. Sew a 3¹/₄"-wide strip of orange print to a 2³/₄"-wide strip of yellow print. Press and cut into 9 segments 2¹/₄" wide to make Unit B.

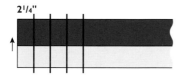

2¹/₄"

Cut 9 segments for Unit B.

4. Sew a gold A piece to a dark green B piece and press to make Unit C. Make 9.

Unit C Make 9.

5. Sew a Unit B to the right side of a Unit C and press to make Section 2. Make 9.

Section 2 Make 9.

6. Sew a 3¹/₄"-wide strip of orange print to a 2³/₄"-wide strip of green with orange small print. Press and cut into 9 segments 3" wide to make Unit D.

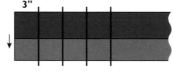

3"

Cut 9 segments for Unit D.

7. Sew a 2¹/₂"-wide strip of dark green print to a 3¹/₂"-wide strip of yellow print. Press and cut into 9 segments 3" wide to make Unit E.

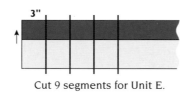

3"

Cut 9 segments for Unit E.

8. Sew a Unit E to the right side of a Unit D to make Section 3. Press. Make 9.

Section 3 Make 9.

9. Sew a 3"-wide strip of light green print to a 3"-wide strip of brown. Make 2 strip sets and press. Cut into 9 segments 5¹/₂" wide to make Section 4.

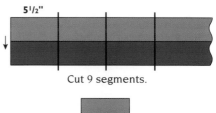

5¹/₂"

Cut 9 segments.

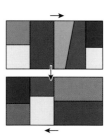

Section 4

10. Sew a Section 1 and 2 together, and sew a Section 3 and 4 together. Press. Sew the 2 halves together to form a complete block. Press. Make 9 blocks.

Make 9.

Complete Block

QUILT ASSEMBLY

1. Referring to the quilt diagram on page 44 and noting how the blocks are rotated, lay out the blocks and sew in rows. Press the seams open.

2. Sew the rows together. Press the seams open.

First Border

Before cutting all final borders, measure your quilt top to confirm measurements for the strip lengths.

1. Cut 2 dark green solid strips $1^1/2$" wide to measure $30^1/2$" long. Sew to top and bottom of the quilt. Press.

2. Cut 2 dark green solid strips $1^1/2$" wide to measure $32^1/2$" long. Sew to sides of the quilt. Press.

Corner Units

1. Draw a diagonal line across the wrong side of the 24 cream $2^1/8$" x $2^1/8$" squares.

2. Place each marked square on an orange solid $2^1/8$" x $2^1/8$" square with right sides together. Sew $1/4$" away from each side of the marked diagonal line. Cut in half on the diagonal line. Press seams open and square up to $1^5/8$" x $1^5/8$". Make 48 half-square triangle units.

Make 24.

$1^5/8$" Half-Square Triangle Unit Make 48.

3. Sew 2 half-square triangle units together, arranging the orange triangles as shown. Add an orange solid 2" triangle to the left side to make Unit A. Press seams open. Make 12.

Unit A Make 12.

4. Sew 2 half-square triangle units together, arranging the orange triangles as shown. Add an orange solid 2" triangle to the right side and a cream square to the left side to make Unit B. Press seams open. Make 12.

Unit B Make 12.

5. Sew a Unit A to the top of a $3^1/8$" yellow and orange triangle. Press. Sew a Unit B to the right side of the $3^1/8$" triangle to make Unit C. Press. Make 12 Unit C's.

Unit C Make 12.

6. Sew a Unit C to the long side of a $5^3/8$" medium olive triangle to complete a block. Press. Make 12 blocks.

Complete Block
Make 12.

Second Border

1. Cut the 4 strips of 5"-wide orange and green large print to measure $23^1/2$" long.

2. Referring to the quilt diagram (page 44) for the rotation of the corner unit blocks, sew blocks to both ends of 2 of the 2nd border strips. Press. Sew to the top and bottom of the quilt. Press.

3. Referring to the quilt diagram, sew 2 blocks to each end of the remaining border strips. Press. Sew to the left and right sides of the quilt. Press.

Kansas Cornstalk Appliqué

1. Trace 3 of each of the appliqué patterns on the paper side of the fusible webbing. (Trace 2 of each pattern piece face up and 1 of each piece face down.)

2. For stalks, cut a strip of paper-backed fusible webbing $2^1/2$" x 20". Fuse the webbing to a $2^1/2$" x 20" strip of medium dark green fabric. Cut 1 strip $3/8$" x $17^1/4$" for Cornstalk 1, 1 strip $3/8$" x $16^1/2$" for Cornstalk 2, and 1 strip $3/8$" x $18^1/2$" for Cornstalk 3. Round one end of each strip for the top of the stalk.

3. Cut 1 strip of paper-backed fusible webbing $4^1/8$" x 6" and fuse to a $4^1/8$" x 6" strip of yellow fabric; cut into 15 strips $1/4$" x $4^1/8$". Round off one end for the top of the corn tassels.

4. Referring to the quilt photo and diagram, place Cornstalk 2 with the leaves and corncobs on the quilt. Center the stalk approximately 12 1/2" from the right side of the quilt and 4 1/2" up from the bottom of the quilt. Before fusing, add yellow corn tassels to the top of the cornstalks. Tuck the ends under the cornstalk and curve the 1/4" strips as shown in the quilt photo. Fuse to the quilt. Use a buttonhole or small zigzag stitch to sew around the edges of the appliqué pieces. The buttonhole stitch may be done by hand or machine.

5. In the same manner, fuse Cornstalk 1, leaves, cobs, and tassels to the quilt. The center of the stalk should be approximately 19 1/4" from the right side of the quilt and 4" up from the bottom of the quilt. The leaves will overlap Cornstalk 2. Buttonhole stitch or zigzag around the edges.

6. In the same manner, fuse Cornstalk 3, leaves, cobs, and tassels to the quilt. The center of the stalk should be approximately 6 1/4" from the right side of the quilt and 2 1/2" up from the bottom of the quilt. The leaves will overlap Cornstalk 2. Buttonhole stitch or zigzag around the edges.

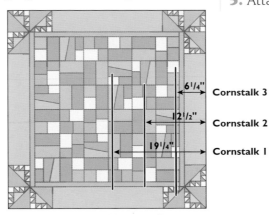

Place cornstalks on quilt.

FINISHING

Refer to Quilting Basics on page 91.

1. Layer the backing, batting, and quilt top; baste.

2. Quilt as desired.

3. Attach a hanging sleeve if desired.

4. Bind or finish as desired.

5. Attach a label.

Quilt Assembly Diagram

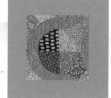

Path in the Wilderness

nderneath the quilt, I put a finger over my lips, telling my seven-year-old cousin, Emory, to be silent. The ladies were quilting for our great-gramma Littleton who was recovering in the hospital from gallstone surgery. The draping queen-size quilt hid us perfectly. He crossed his eyes at me behind his thick glasses.

At eight years old, I was convinced that adults knew all sorts of wonderful secrets that they deliberately kept from us kids, like a snippet I'd heard this morning about a girl at church when I wandered past my great-aunt Garnet's bedroom.

"Poor thing, she sounds confused," said my gramma Dove. She and I were visiting Arkansas from California where we lived on my dad's cattle ranch. We were spending a month here in Sugartree, the place where I was born, because Dove didn't want me to lose my Southern roots.

"What goes around, comes around," Aunt Garnet said cryptically.

"Pretty stones and glass houses, Sister," Dove said. It was one of her favorite sayings, one she tossed at me whenever I made fun of someone else.

"In this particular case that doesn't apply," Aunt Garnet said. "I'd never do what Bobbie Mae did."

"We'd like to think we couldn't be carried away by passion, but who knows . . . ?"

Passion? That sounded intriguing. Certainly more interesting than *My Friend Flicka*, which I'd already read three times this week. Passion and all its mysteries were just starting to interest me.

"Think what you like, but I'd never do what she did," Aunt Garnet said.

Dove clucked under her breath. It meant she didn't agree with you but was choosing not to argue.

Then they started talking about Dove's chickens and what kind of feed she was using.

"We have to find out about Bobbie Mae's passion," I told Emory later that morning when we sat in his tree house sipping from RC Cola bottles filled with Hawaiian Punch. He was eating his third Moonpie. We stole a box of them from his pantry because his mama was sick and his daddy worked all the time, so Emory ran around, as Aunt Garnet said, like a crazy wild Indian. Emory lived in a big brick house right behind Aunt Garnet's two-story house where Dove and I were staying.

"Why?" he asked.

"Because I want to know. A bunch of ladies from the church are coming to work on a quilt for great-gramma Littleton this afternoon. Maybe they'll talk about it."

"She's *old*," Emory said. We thought she looked like one of the Bible characters from Sunday School.

"The quilt's called *Path in the Wilderness*. She told Dove that's what her life has always been so the pattern is perfect." Emory eyed another Moonpie.

"We can sneak in and hide under the quilt. The sides will hide us," I said. "Maybe they'll talk about Bobbie Mae."

He blinked like an owl behind his thick glasses. "Who cares? I'd rather go catch frogs down at the creek."

"Go ahead, but when I find out, I'm not going to tell you."

■ Here is my great-aunt's *Path in the Wilderness* quilt about which Benni speaks to Emory in *Kansas Troubles*. Margrit designed a beautiful and fun pattern that matches this quilt.

So that's how we ended up underneath the quilt, trying to breathe quietly and hear what passionate thing Bobbie Mae Willard did that, as Aunt Garnet said, shocked the living daylights out of everyone at Sugartree Baptist Church.

It didn't take them long to bring it up once the quilting started. Emory and I looked up and watched the needles go in and out as fast as they talked.

"I always thought Bobbie Mae was a pretty little thing," Mrs. Mackey said. She was the youngest deacon's wife and smelled like roses. "Those green Irish eyes."

"Them eyes is what got her in hot water to begin with," said Velma Mungers, who sewed for a living. "She couldn't keep 'em to herself."

"Oh, Velma," Dove said. "She's young and foolish. I think we've all been there once or twice."

"Pregnant with her own brother-in-law's child!" Aunt Garnet said. "Her mama Ronella will never live it down."

I looked wide-eyed at Emory.

"The divorce was almost final so it's not quite as bad as it sounds," Mrs. Mackey said. "He is almost technically not her brother-in-law anymore. And they are getting married."

Velma Mungers lowered her voice. "I heard Bobbie Mae and Ricky got together a few times during their separation."

"At least Ronella knows any child Bobbie Mae has is really her grandchild," said Mrs. Mackey with a giggle.

"Family gatherings will certainly be interesting in that household," said Mrs. Doolittle, who owned the dime store in town. She was sometimes nice, sometimes cranky, depending on whether her husband was drinking.

"At least they're keeping it in the family," Dove said, amicably.

"Pastor's about ready to pop a blood vessel," Mrs. Doolittle said.

"I'll just bet," Dove said. "Though there's at least ten sermons he could get out of it."

Emory took a sip of his Hawaiian Punch, and I scowled at him.

"I told you not to bring that," I mouthed at him.

He stuck his red tongue at me and took another drink.

"Frankly," Mrs. Doolittle said, "I say tie their little noodles in a knot at birth and save us all a lot of grief."

Her remark caught Emory by surprise, and he sprayed his mouthful of red punch all over me, the quilt, and the ladies' feet.

The women screamed and jumped up. Aunt Garnet's voice yelled, "Emory Delano Littleton!"

Emory looked like he was ready to cry. He was scared to death of Aunt Garnet. I grabbed the bottle of punch and crawled out from under the quilt.

"It's not Emory, it's me," I said, holding the offending bottle in my hand and taking a drink to seal my guilt.

"Young lady, you should be ashamed," Aunt Garnet said.

"Yes, ma'am," I said, glancing over at Dove, who winked at me.

"We all better go clean up our feet," Dove said, herding the other women toward the kitchen.

As she passed me, she whispered, "Tell Emory to skedaddle when we're in the kitchen."

"Yes, ma'am," I said.

"And," she added, "I think it's about time you and me had a little talk about the birds and the bees."

■ Another barn

Path in the Wilderness

Designed by Margrit Hall
Made by Cathryn Tallman-Evans
Quilted by Ginny Jaranowski

Finished Block Size: 7½"
Finished Quilt Size: 45" x 60"
Fabric graciously supplied by The Fabric Patch Quilt Shop.

FABRICS AND CUTTING

Template patterns are located on page 49.

FABRIC COLOR	FABRIC AMOUNT	CUTTING DIRECTIONS
Green	2³/₈ yards	Cut 20 strips 3¹/₄" wide, then cut into 96 E's. Cut 6 strips 2¹/₄" wide for binding.
Reds	¹/₄ yard **each** of 5 reds	Cut 2 strips 3¹/₂" wide of each red, then cut into a total of 96 D's.
Variety of Colors	2¹/₂ to 3 yards total of 10–12 fabrics	Cut 1 strip 3³/₄" wide of each color, then cut into a total of 96 A's. Cut 2 strips 2¹/₂" wide of each color, then cut into a total of 96 B's and 48 C's.
Backing	2⁷/₈ yards	Piece horizontally.

Press seams in the direction of the arrows, unless otherwise indicated.

BLOCK ASSEMBLY

1. Using a variety of colors in a random placement, sew 2 A's, 2 B's, and 1 C together to make Section 1. Press. Make 48.

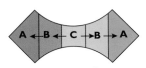

Section 1 Make 48.

2. Fold an E and a D in half to find the centers, and finger press to create a center crease. Place D and E right sides together with D (convex curve) on the bottom and E (concave curve) on the top. Match the centers and pin, then match and pin the outer edges of the curve. Continue to pin along the curve, clipping the concave curve of E to ease as necessary. Sew carefully. Open and press. Make 96.

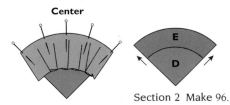

Section 2 Make 96.

3. Sew Section 2's to each side of a Section 1. Make sure Section 1 is on top of Section 2 with right sides together. Make 48.

Center

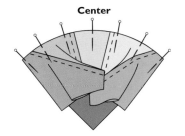

Complete Block Make 48.

QUILT ASSEMBLY

1. Lay out the blocks using the diagram as a guide, then sew the blocks together in rows. Press the seams of rows in alternating directions.

2. Sew the rows together and press.

FINISHING

Refer to Quilting Basics on page 91.

1. Layer the backing, batting, and quilt top; baste.

2. Quilt as desired.

3. Attach a hanging sleeve if desired.

4. Bind or finish as desired.

5. Attach a label.

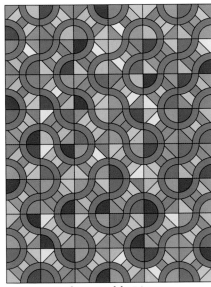

Quilt Assembly Diagram

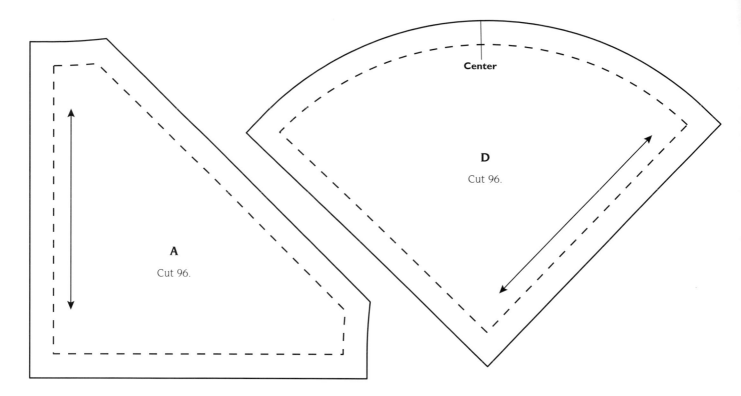

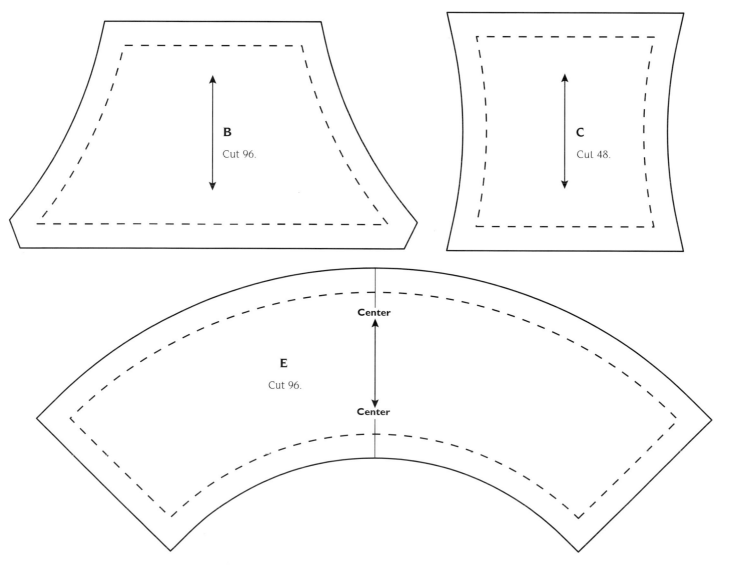

Path in the Wilderness

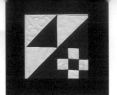

Best Friends in Spite Of

"I couldn't stand you," I said, laughing at my best friend, Elvia Aragon, as I pointed to our picture in an album I was putting back up on a shelf. She'd had the walls in her townhouse painted three weeks ago and was just now getting things put away. With her job as manager of Blind Harry's Bookstore and my seven-month-old second marriage to Gabe Ortiz, San Celina's police chief, we'd not had much time to visit, so this was killing two birds with one stone.

"I thought you were a terror," Elvia said, laughing with me. I handed her the first picture we had taken together in Mrs. Goldstein's second-grade class.

She took the picture and grimaced at her shiny black Dutch-boy bob. "Look at my hair."

"I think it's cute."

We stopped and sat down on her queen-sized bed. It was covered with a pale almond down comforter and lacy pillows crocheted by her mother.

"Remember the first thing you said to me?" I mimicked her long-ago little girl soprano. "Benni Ramsey, did you know that the ribbons in your hair do *not* match the red in your skirt? They are maroon and your skirt is red." I laughed. "You were such a little prissy pants."

Elvia narrowed her dark eyes, studying the photo. We stood next to each other in the group shot, front row middle, the two shortest girls in class. I sported an impressive black-and-blue eye, one I'd gotten only hours before. I remember thinking my gramma Dove was going to kill me for messing up my school picture.

"Then you spit at me!" she said. "If I was a prissy pants, you were an uncivilized hooligan."

"Hooligan?" Giggling, I tossed a pillow at her. "You've been reading too much Jane Austen."

She caught the pillow and hugged it to her chest. "I said that because I was so jealous of you."

I leaned toward her, surprised by her confession. "You were jealous of *me?*"

She tossed the pillow aside and reached over to pick up an emery board from the white and gold nightstand. She concentrated on filing an already perfect thumbnail. "You were just so . . . accepted. Everyone knew you and liked you. You weren't afraid of anything or anyone."

"Me? *You* are the most confident, fearless person I know!"

She looked up at me, her dark eyes serious. "Not back then. I'll never forget how you stood up to that bully. What was his name?"

"Mark Johnston. His family owned the ranch over the hill from ours. The one that Jack's dad bought. What a little jerk that kid was."

During recess on the day of our class photos, Mark Johnston and two other boys had cornered her in the back of the field. As she clung terrified to the chain link fence, they pelted her with dirt clods, calling her "monkey" and "greaser." Without hesitation, I jumped on Mark Johnston's back and started pounding his head, my surprise attack causing the other boys to scatter. I ended up with a black eye, but also gave Mark one and a fat lip besides.

Elvia held my hazel eyes with her dark ones. "Did I ever thank you?"

I made a silly face at her. "You were seven years old! I think you might have given me a Twinkie at lunch."

■ Breakfast is a very popular meal in San Luis Obispo County (nicknamed SLO—as in "slow down!"). Although Liddie's Café in San Celina doesn't actually exist, this could have been a sign in Liddie's window.

She shook her head, her glossy hair catching the overhead light. "You would remember that."

"Best kind of thank you for a second grader."

"Anyway, thank you, *mi amiga*."

"You've paid it back a million times. You were there when I married Jack and when he died, when I married Gabe, and all the times I've screwed up and been hurt. You've always been there for me when I needed you. One little shiner is small potatoes compared with that."

She sighed. "Papa was the one who wanted me to attend public school instead of Catholic school. He told Mama it would toughen me up." She shivered slightly in her pale blue sweater.

"It worked," I pointed out. She'd turned Blind Harry's into one of the most successful independent bookstores in California. She was a respected and sometimes intimidating member of San Celina's business community.

"Maybe. But, right now I feel like that frightened second grader. What if I fail? What if . . . " She paused for a moment. "What if the store is all I end up ever having?"

Her normally unemotional face held that same terrified look I remembered from second grade. We never talked much about how little she dated, how she seemed incapable of having a relationship with a man, whether she was jealous that I'd not only been married once, but twice.

I scooted across the bed to her and took her hands in mine. "Your Prince Charming is out there, Elvia. I promise."

She laughed and squeezed my hands. "I doubt that."

I raised my eyebrows at her, only halfway teasing. "My cousin Emory in Arkansas still asks after you."

She let go of my hands and said, "I know you love him, Benni, but Prince Charming he isn't."

"Trust me, he would have taken on those bullies too."

She shrugged and changed the subject. "I've always wondered what Dove said when you came home with a black eye?"

I grinned. "After I told her what happened, she hugged me, baked me my favorite chocolate-walnut pie, and let me eat a big piece *before* supper."

Elvia laughed. "I guess the nut really doesn't fall far from the tree."

I tried one more time. "Emory's part of that tough ole Southern tree too."

She just rolled her eyes and smiled.

■ Mission San Luis Obispo de Tolosa in downtown San Luis Obispo. It was fifth in the chain of 21 missions. I based my Santa Celine Mission on this building.

■ This bronze sculpture and fountain is in front of the Mission San Luis Obispo.

Best Friends in Spite Of

Designed by Margrit Hall
Made by Judith Rhodes
Quilted by Kathleen Pappas and Phyllis Reddish

Finished Block Size: 11¼"
Finished Quilt Size: 47¾" x 47¾"
Fabric graciously supplied by RJR Fabrics.

FABRICS AND CUTTING

Template patterns are located on the pullout.

FABRIC COLOR	FABRIC AMOUNT	CUTTING DIRECTIONS
White	$2^1/4$ yards	**Goose in the Pond block** Cut 3 strips $3^1/4$" wide, then cut into 30 squares $3^1/4$" x $3^1/4$". Cut 2 strips $2^3/4$" wide, then cut into 25 squares $2^3/4$" x $2^3/4$". Cut 8 strips $1^1/4$" wide. **Schoolhouse block** Cut 3 strips 2" wide, then cut into 4 B's, 4 C's, 4 rectangles 2" x $5^1/2$", and 8 rectangles 2" x $2^1/4$". Cut 1 strip 4" wide. Fold strip in half, wrong sides together, and cut 4 pairs of D's (4 D's and 4 Dr's). Each cut equals 1 pair. Cut 1 strip $1^5/8$" wide, then cut into 4 F's. Cut 1 strip $1^3/4$" wide, then cut into 4 rectangles $1^3/4$" x $5^1/4$". Cut 1 strip $1^1/2$" wide, then cut into 4 rectangles $1^1/2$" x $4^1/4$", 8 rectangles $1^1/2$" x $1^7/8$", and 4 rectangles $1^1/2$" x $1^1/4$". **Sashing and Border** Cut 8 strips $1^3/4$" wide, then cut 2 of the strips into 6 rectangles $1^3/4$" x $11^3/4$". (Set the remaining strips aside.) Cut 6 strips 2" wide.
Red	$2^1/4$ yards	**Goose in the Pond block** Cut 3 strips $3^1/4$" wide, then cut into 30 squares $3^1/4$" x $3^1/4$". Cut 7 strips $1^1/4$" wide. **Schoolhouse block** Cut 2 strips 4" wide, then cut into 4 E's and 4 G's. Cut 1 strip 2" wide, then cut into 4 rectangles 2" x $1^3/4$", 8 rectangles 2" x $7/8$" and 4 A's. Cut 2 strips $1^3/4$" wide, then cut into 8 rectangles $1^3/4$" x $4^1/4$" and 12 rectangles $1^3/4$" x $3^1/4$". Cut 2 strips $1^1/2$" wide, then cut into 8 rectangles $1^1/2$" x 7" and 4 rectangles $1^1/2$" x 4". Cut 1 strip $1^3/8$" wide, then cut into 16 rectangles $1^3/8$" x $1^7/8$". Cut 1 strip $1^1/4$" wide, then cut into 8 rectangles $1^1/4$" x $3/4$". **Border and Binding** Cut 10 strips 2" wide for border. Cut 5 strips $2^1/4$" wide for binding.
Backing	3 yards	Piece together.

Press seams in the direction of the arrows, unless otherwise indicated.

 GOOSE IN THE POND BLOCK ASSEMBLY

1. Draw a diagonal line across the wrong side of each white 3¹/₄" x 3¹/₄" square.

2. Place each marked square on a red 3¹/₄" x 3¹/₄" square with right sides together. Sew ¹/₄" from each side of the marked diagonal line. Cut in half along the diagonal line. Press seams open and square up to 2³/₄" square. Make 60 half-square triangle units.

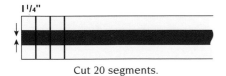

Make 30.

Make 60.

3. Sew a white 1¹/₄" strip to each side of a 1¹/₄" red strip. Make 3 white/red/white strip sets. Cut into 20 segments 2³/₄" wide and 20 segments 1¹/₄" wide. Press.

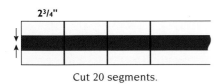

2³/₄"

Cut 20 segments.

1¹/₄"

Cut 20 segments.

4. Sew a red 1¹/₄" strip to each side of a 1¹/₄" white strip. Make 2 red/white/red strips. Cut into 40 segments 1¹/₄" wide. Press.

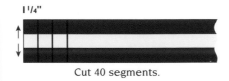

1¹/₄"

Cut 40 segments.

5. Sew white/red/white and red/white/red 1¹/₄" segments together to make a Nine-Patch block. Press. Make 20 Nine-Patch blocks.

Make 20.

6. Sew 2 half-square triangle units to each side of a white 2³/₄" x 2³/₄" square to make Unit 1. Press. Make 10.

Unit 1 Make 10.

7. Sew a half-square triangle unit to each side of a white 2³/₄" x 2³/₄" square to make Unit 2. Press. Make 10.

Unit 2 Make 10.

8. Sew a nine-patch unit to each side of a 2³/₄" white/red/white segment to make Unit 3. Press. Make 10.

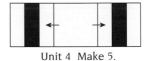

Unit 3 Make 10.

9. Sew a 2³/₄" white/red/white segment to each side of a white 2³/₄" x 2³/₄" square to make Unit 4. Press. Make 5.

Unit 4 Make 5.

10. Sew units together to make 5 Goose in the Pond blocks. Press seams open.

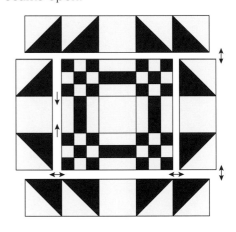

Goose in the Pond Block Make 5.

◥ SCHOOLHOUSE BLOCK ASSEMBLY

1. Sew B and C to A to make Section 1. Press. Make 4.

Section 1 Make 4.

2. Sew ³/₄" x 1¹/₄" red rectangles to the top and bottom of a 1¹/₂" x 1¹/₄" white square. Press. Sew ⁷/₈" x 2" red rectangles to the sides and press to make the bell tower unit. Make 4.

Make 4.

3. Sew 2 white 2" x 2¹/₄" rectangles, 1 white 2" x 5¹/₂" rectangle, 1 red 1³/₄" x 2" rectangle, and the bell tower unit together to make Section 2. Press. Make 4.

Section 2 Make 4

4. Sew D, E, F, G, and Dr together to make Section 3. Press. Make 4.

Section 3 Make 4.

5. Sew 2 red 1³/₄" x 4¹/₄" rectangles to the sides of a white 1¹/₂" x 4¹/₄" rectangle. Press. Sew a red 1¹/₂" x 4" rectangle to the top and press to make the door unit. Make 4.

Door Unit Make 4.

6. Sew 2 red 1³/₈" x 1⁷/₈" rectangles to the top and bottom of a white 1¹/₂" x 1⁷/₈" rectangle to make a window. Press. Make 8.

Window Make 8.

7. Sew 3 red 1³/₄" x 3¹/₄" rectangles to the sides of the windows. Press. Make 4.

Make 4.

8. Sew 2 red 1¹/₂" x 7" rectangles to the top and bottom to make the window unit. Press. Make 4.

Window Unit Make 4.

9. Sew a white 1³/₄" x 5¹/₄" rectangle between the window and door units to make Section 4. Press. Make 4.

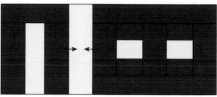

Section 4 Make 4.

10. Sew Sections 1, 2, 3, and 4 together to complete the Schoolhouse block. Press seams open. Make 4. The unfinished block should measure 11³/₄".

Schoolhouse Block Make 4.

QUILT ASSEMBLY

First Border and Sashing

Before cutting all final borders, measure your quilt top to confirm measurements for the strip lengths.

1. Sew $1^3/4$" x $11^3/4$" sashing strips between the blocks. Press.

2. Cut 4 of the white $1^3/4$" strips to measure $36^3/4$" long. Sew strips between rows and to the top and bottom of the quilt. Press.

3. Cut 2 of the white $1^3/4$" strips to measure $39^1/4$" long. Sew strips to the sides of the quilt. Press.

Second Border

1. Sew red 2" strips to each side of a white 2" strip. Make 4 red/white/red strip sets. Press toward the red strips. Cut each strip set to measure $39^1/4$" long for the 2nd borders. Press.

2. Sew 2 of the 2nd borders to the top and bottom of the quilt. Press.

Corner Nine-Patch Unit Assembly

Note: See diagrams on page 54 for the nine-patch unit construction technique.

1. Cut 2 of the white 2" strips and 2 of the red 2" strips into 4 strips 2" x 20" each.

2. Sew white 2" x 20" strips to each side of a red 2" x 20" strip. Press toward the red strip. Cut strip set into 8 segments 2" wide. Sew red 2" x 20" strips to each side of a white 2" x 20" strip. Press toward the red strips. Cut into 4 segments 2" wide. Sew segments together to make a Nine-Patch corner unit. Press. Make 4.

3. Sew a corner unit on both ends of the remaining 2nd border units and press seams open. Sew to the sides of the quilt. Press.

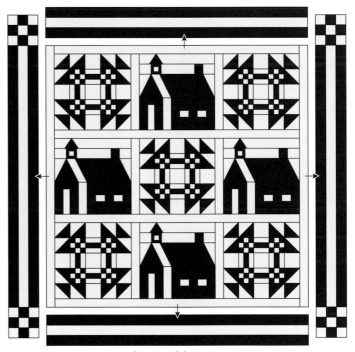

Quilt Assembly Diagram

FINISHING

Refer to Quilting Basics on page 91.

1. Layer the backing, batting, and quilt top; baste.

2. Quilt as desired.

3. Attach a hanging sleeve if desired.

4. Bind or finish as desired.

5. Attach a label.

It's Never Too Late to Be a Cowgirl

"Oh, Daddy, I love him!"

I gazed into the stall at the Appaloosa gelding with the big yellow bow around his neck. I walked over and held out my palm, letting the horse inhale my scent and get accustomed to me. He blew air and nibbled at my hand. His eyes gave me an alert but kind look. I knew at that moment this horse would be with me forever.

A pleased, pink-tinged expression came over my dad's face. Even though I was thirty-five, he was still embarrassed when he gave me gifts.

"Well, pumpkin," he said, "I saw him up in Salinas and couldn't resist. He looks just like old Missy, don't you think?"

Missy was my first horse, a gentle Appaloosa mare who had the easy-going personality of a golden retriever. A picture of her wearing a straw hat and a garland of wilted daisies and wild roses hung in my bedroom. It was taken when I was ten years old and rode her in the San Celina May Day parade. I had meant for the garland to look like the kind that racehorses won. It ended up making her look like exactly what she was, a young girl's beloved first horse. I'd ridden her since I was five, and when she died from colic twelve years later, I thought my heart would break. I'd owned many horses since then, but none of them touched my soul like Missy.

I ran my hand down the horse's neck. "What's his name?"

"José."

"José?" I'd never heard of a horse named José.

He shrugged. "That's what the man said."

I walked over to the grain barrel and stuck my hand in the sweet smelling mix. José cleaned my hand as efficiently as a cat.

"Hey, hey, José," I crooned softly. "You're going to like it here at the Ramsey Ranch. You know, they call California's central coast cow heaven. But it's horse heaven too."

He nibbled at my hand, searching for more grain. Then his head moved up and down as if he were agreeing with me. I reached up and scratched between his ears, something Missy had loved, but not all horses do. His eyes glazed over in ecstasy.

"He's a good little cow pony," Daddy said, pushing his straw Stetson back on his head. "Has a nice, quiet manner."

"Let's take him out to the ring," I said, opening the stable door. Daddy went into the tack room to fetch my saddle.

In the ring, I rode him around a few times, getting used to him and letting him get used to me. Just like Missy though, he and I seemed to bond immediately. I knew we would be together until one of us was no longer on this earth.

■ Here I am on Henry in front of—what else?—an oak tree.

■ I bought these boots at the Boot Barn in Paso Robles. They are the perfect boots, in my opinion—fancy on top and plain on the bottom.

■ These boots were a steal at the Justin Boot Outlet in Texas. Even Benni, who hates to shop, would love that store.

I rode up to my dad, who stood at the railing, his tanned forearms resting on the top rung.

"I wish Jack could have seen him," I said, feeling sad for a moment. "He would have gone nuts." Jack, my childhood sweetheart and first husband, loved horses as much as I did.

I'd never seen anyone connect with animals like Jack did. Even the scared, new heifers giving birth for the first time immediately calmed down when they heard his voice, a soft, soothing Texas drawl.

"I know," Daddy said, looking down at his hands. Talking about Jack, even though he'd been gone for almost two years, was hard for my dad.

"Hey, what's going on out here?"

We turned to look at the long-legged man who strode toward us, his black hair shiny as a crow's wing.

My heart jumped a little, and José stirred underneath me, feeling my excitement. He could already read my feelings like Missy had.

"It's okay, boy," I said, patting his neck. "He's definitely a friend."

I watched my husband of less than a year come toward us. He was a tall, blue-eyed Hispanic man who had the confident air of a police officer, which made sense, because that was exactly what he was. Daddy turned around and, when Gabe reached him, held out his hand. The two men I loved most in the world. Though I missed Jack still, my heart at that moment felt so full, I thought it would explode.

When Jack died almost two years ago, too young at thirty-four, I thought my life had ended, that I'd received my share of happiness and used it up early, like gulping down your piece of birthday cake and realizing that you wouldn't get another. But then this bold, ocean-eyed police chief barged into my life, turning it upside down with his whispered Spanish words and his irrepressible smile.

It reminded me of something my gramma Dove once said to a missionary lady who was visiting us. The missionary had never ridden a horse in her life, though she'd always wanted to. Dove took it upon herself to give the woman, who was in her late 60s, her first riding lesson.

"I couldn't," the lady said, looking longingly at Missy. "I'm too old. It's too late."

"It's never too late to be a cowgirl," Dove said firmly and had the woman trotting around the ring in less than an hour.

I looked over at my new husband and felt a swell of love. Dove was right. It was never too late to be a cowgirl . . . or to fall in love again.

"Hey, Gabriel Ortiz," I called. "Come over here and meet José. You aren't the only sexy Latino man in my life now."

He grinned and opened the gate, walking toward me and the rest of our life.

■ Cattle are still prominent in SLO County. Benni's father calls it "cow heaven" because of the temperate weather and good pasture land.

■ Another towering oak tree; both humans and cattle alike seek the cool shade on warm days.

■ Another cow looking for a drink of water

It's Never Too Late to Be a Cowgirl

Designed by Margrit Hall

Made by Tami Taylor

Quilted by Phyllis Reddish

Finished Quilt Size: 39" x 39"

Fabric graciously donated by Rainbow Fabrics.

⌂ FABRICS AND CUTTING

Template patterns are located on the pullout.

FABRIC COLOR	FABRIC AMOUNT	CUTTING DIRECTIONS
Cream	1^1/$_4$ yards	Cut 1 square 11^1/$_2$" x 11^1/$_2$". Cut 2 squares 10^1/$_8$" x 10^1/$_8$", then cut each square once on the diagonal to make 4 triangles. Cut 2 squares 14^3/$_4$" x 14^3/$_4$", then cut each square once on the diagonal to make 4 triangles. Cut 1 strip 6" wide, then cut into 4 squares 6" x 6".
Dark Teal	^{7}/$_8$ yard	Cut 4 strips 6" wide for outside border.
Dark Brown	^{1}/$_4$ yard	Cut 2 strips 1^1/$_2$" wide, then cut into 2 strips 1^1/$_2$" x 11^1/$_2$" and 2 strips 1^1/$_2$" x 13^1/$_2$". Cut 4 N's and 4 S's.
Red	^{3}/$_8$ yard	Cut 2 strips 1" wide, then cut into 2 strips 1" x 20" and 2 strips 1" x 19". Cut 1 A.
Light Red	4" x 4^1/$_2$" scrap	Cut 1 B (or 1 rectangle 3^1/$_2$" x 3^3/$_4$").
Black	^{3}/$_8$ yard	Cut 4 strips 2^1/$_2$" wide for binding. Cut 1 F.
Off-White	Scrap	Cut 2 D's, 1 E, and 1 C (or 1 square 1^1/$_2$" x 1^1/$_2$").
Tan	Scrap	Cut 1 G and 4 J's.
Dark Aqua	4" x 4" scrap	Cut 2 H's.
Dark Pink	4" x 4" scrap	Cut 2 H's.
Light Aqua	1^1/$_2$" x 5" scrap	Cut 2 I's.
Light Pink	1^1/$_2$" x 5" scrap	Cut 2 I's.
Gray	^{1}/$_4$ yard	Cut 8 K's and 8 T's.
Dark Green	4^1/$_2$" x 10" scrap	Cut 2 L's, 2 O's, and 4 Q's.
Dark Purple	4^1/$_2$" x 10" scrap	Cut 2 L's, 2 O's, and 4 Q's.
Light Green	4" x 8" scrap	Cut 2 M's and 2 P's.
Light Purple	4" x 8" scrap	Cut 2 M's and 2 P's.
Dark Orange	^{1}/$_8$ yard	Cut 12 R's.
Medium Brown	^{1}/$_4$ yard	Cut 4 S's.
Light Brown	^{1}/$_4$ yard	Cut 4 S's.
Backing	1^1/$_4$ yards	Piece together.
Paper-Backed Fusible Webbing	1^1/$_2$ yards	

Other materials: thread for machine appliqué

Press seams in the direction of the arrows, unless otherwise indicated.

⬛ FUSIBLE APPLIQUÉ

See Quilting Basics on page 92.

1. Trace patterns face up (unless otherwise indicated) on the paper side of the fusible webbing. Cut around the pattern, leaving about ¼" all around. Following the manufacturer's instructions, fuse to the back side of the fabric.

2. Cut the fabric on the drawn line. Remove the paper and fuse fabric shape to the background in alphabetical sequence. Use the quilt photo on page 59 and diagram on page 62 as placement guides.

3. Topstitch or buttonhole stitch around appliqué.

⬛ QUILT ASSEMBLY

1. To make Unit A, fuse pieces A, B, C, D, E, F, and G to the center 11½" x 11½" square.

Unit A

■ This is what the Harper and Ramsey ranches would look like.

2. To make Unit B, fuse H, I, J, and K to the 10⅛" triangles. Make 4: 2 with aqua hats and 2 with pink hats.

Unit B Make 4.

3. To make Unit C, fuse L, M, N, O, P, Q, and R to the 14¾" triangles. Make 4: 2 with green boots and 2 with purple boots.

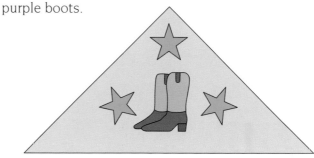

Unit C Make 4 total.

4. To make Unit D, fuse 2 T's to a 6" x 6" square overlapping the horseshoes at the dotted lines and centering on the diagonal of the square. Make 4.

Unit D Make 4.

■ These are a favorite pair (out of 25) because they go with everything.
Brown and black are the only two colors of boots acceptable to most working cowgirls, though they often like red for special occasions.

5. To make the horse border, fold the border strip in half to find the center. (Do not cut the strip to size until after the quilt is constructed.) Match the center of the medium brown horse S to the center of the strip. Place the dark brown and light brown horses approximately 1³/₄" from the center horse and fuse. Make 4.

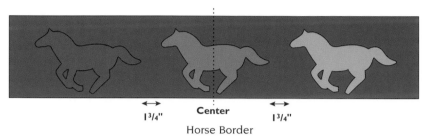

Center
1³/₄"   1³/₄"
Horse Border

6. Sew the 1¹/₂" x 11¹/₂" dark brown strips to opposite sides of Unit A. Press.
7. Sew the 1¹/₂" x 13¹/₂" dark brown strips to the remaining sides of Unit A to make Section 1. Press.
8. Sew Unit B's to opposite sides of Section 1. Press and then sew Unit B's to the 2 remaining sides to make Section 2. Press.

Quilt Assembly Diagram

9. Sew the red 1" x 19" strips to opposite sides of Section 2. Press and then sew the red 1" x 20" strips to the 2 remaining sides to make Section 3. Press.
10. Sew Unit C's to opposite sides of a Section 3. Press and then sew Unit C's to the 2 remaining sides of Section 3 to make the quilt body. Press.

BORDERS

Before cutting all final borders, measure your quilt top to confirm measurements for the strip lengths.
1. Fold horse borders in half, down the center of the medium brown horse.
2. Cut folded borders to measure 14¹/₄" long (28¹/₂" total).
3. Sew a horse border to the top and bottom of the quilt. Press.
4. Sew Unit D corner squares to each end of the remaining 2 horse borders. Press and sew to the sides of the quilt. Press.

FINISHING

Refer to Quilting Basics on page 91.
1. Layer the backing, batting, and quilt top; baste.
2. Quilt as desired.
3. Attach a hanging sleeve if desired.
4. Bind or finish as desired.
5. Attach a label.

Final Roundup

"I'm going for a walk," Dove said. It was a late autumn afternoon at their ranch outside San Celina. The sky was that particular shade of shimmery clear blue that gave the golden hills a burnished, metallic look that almost hurt your eyes.

"Do you want company?" her granddaughter Benni asked. They'd all said good-bye to Dove's fellow, as she liked to called him, Isaac Lyons, after a belly-splitting Sunday dinner of pot roast, new potatoes, fresh green beans, late tomatoes, and a chocolate-pecan pie that made all the men in the room—Isaac, Dove's son Ben, and Benni's husband, Gabe—give a groan of pleasure with every bite.

"No, thanks, honeybun," she said, gazing with affection at her oldest grandchild, who was lying on the sofa with her head in her handsome husband's lap. His fingers played with her curly hair, unable to keep his hands off her even after a year and a half of marriage. Their passion for each other is what sparked a ray of hope in Dove for her and Isaac. "You let your dinner settle. I just need a little time to myself."

The truth was she needed some time to try and figure out what she should do with all these complex feelings she had about Isaac, a huge polar bear of a man who made her heart flutter like a teenager. She never in a million dog's years ever expected to fall in love again after her first husband died over thirty years ago. She certainly never expected to feel like this when she was almost seventy-seven!

She walked down the long driveway, following the wooden fence rail, and turned off on a path that led to a small creek running through the ranch where she'd come to live when Benni was six.

Oh Lord, that was a sad, sad year. It was springtime when she and her youngest son, Arnie, arrived on the train from Arkansas. Her oldest son, Ben, stood on the platform waiting for them, clutching Benni's six-year-old hand. Benni wore a little red cowgirl hat and tiny black boots. The moment she saw Dove, she threw herself in her arms, holding on like Dove was the only thing that would keep her from flying away. When Dove saw the house, how Ben had been trying to keep it up, nurse his dying wife, take care of his baby daughter, and maintain the ranch, she understood why Benni grabbed onto her like she was the Rock of Gibraltar.

It took Dove a few weeks, but she got everyone settled down and on a schedule. The relief on her daughter-in-law Alice's face when Dove walked into the dusty, stale-smelling bedroom made Dove want to flat out start bawling. But there'd been no time for tears. She had a family to take care of. And she had for the last thirty years. Benni was grown now, married again after the tragic loss of her young husband, Jack. Happy again.

Lord, thank you for that, Dove prayed as she walked. And for a million other things besides.

She reached the creek and walked to her favorite spot, a smooth rock that she came to every day when she first arrived at the ranch, when everyone's overwhelming needs seemed too much for her. She'd talk to God on this rock, spill

■ Old windmills are slowly disappearing as rural life is being replaced by housing tracts.

out all of her fears and anger and doubts. She wet this rock with tears more times than she could count. Endless drops of tears for all the hard times her family endured.

"Hello, Lord, nice to talk to you again," she said, settling down on her rock. "It was a real nice day. I surely thank you for it. The food was real good, even if I did prepare it myself. I thank you for your bounty and for giving me the strength to make something of it." She looked out over the creek, where the late afternoon sun caused bursts of light to dance across the surface, reminding Dove of the Fourth of July sparklers Benni still loved. "Okay, Father, let's get down to brass tacks here because I've got to feed some calves in a little bit. This man, Isaac, just what were you thinking, bringing him into my life? I mean, honestly, do you realize how old I am? I'm about ready for the final roundup and you send this man to make me think about, well, you know. You have got to be kidding."

She paused a moment. From her long relationship with God, she knew sometimes the answers came in that still, small voice inside you. That you had to get still to hear it, something she thought young people today just didn't quite grasp with how much noise they toted around with their cell phones, CD players, and such.

Behind her, a tree rustled, and a mourning dove shook out its wings, then let out a soft call to its mate.

"Okay, I suppose you know what's what," she said, wrapping her hands around one knee. "Like I've always tried to do, I want to lead my life how you want me to, so give me some kind of sign, if you don't mind, and let me know if I should be staying with this man or telling him to hit the road."

Again, she didn't really expect an answer. She knew, like all the things that had happened in her life, He always, eventually, made His will known. When the time was right, she'd receive her answer.

She stood up, lifted up her hands in praise. "Thank you, Sir, for this beautiful, beautiful land. For your grace and for your love. And for your perfect plan even when you don't share with me what it is. Now I'd better go get those calves fed. Amen."

She took one last look at her beloved creek, her eye catching a bright flash in the water. Her hand reached toward the flash, her fingers grasping a rock right below the water's surface. She inspected it, the water dripping down her hand. It was smooth as glass, shaped like a heart. There was one tiny chip in the center.

She cradled the rock in the palm of her hand, looked up to the sky, and let out a great, joyful laugh that echoed through the trees, the hills, and up to the heavens themselves.

■ I often rode up to the top of the Fitzhugh ranch with my friend Joy and her parents, Abbott and Lorna.

■ One of the Fitzhugh bulls known affectionately as "Creampuff," though he was often anything but!

Final Roundup

Designed by Margrit Hall
Made by Vicki Hoskins
Quilted by Kathleen Pappas

Finished Block Size: 6"
Finished Quilt Size: 59" x 71"
Fabric graciously supplied by RJR Fabrics.

◆ FABRICS AND CUTTING

Dove template pattern is located on page 69.

FABRIC COLOR	FABRIC AMOUNT	CUTTING DIRECTIONS
Cream	$3/4$ yard	Cut 1 square $17^1/2$" x $17^1/2$". Cut 1 strip $3^3/8$" wide, then cut into 3 squares $3^3/8$" x $3^3/8$". Cut each square twice on the diagonal to make 12 quarter-square triangles. Cut the remainder of the strip to $2^1/2$" wide, then cut into 4 squares $2^1/2$" x $2^1/2$".
Dark Red with Black	$1/4$ yard	Cut 2 A's. (If using needleturn appliqué, trace A on the front of fabric and cut $1/4$" outside the drawn line.)
Medium Red with Cream	$1/4$ yard	Cut 2 A's. (If using needleturn appliqué, trace A on the front of fabric and cut $1/4$" outside the drawn line.)
Light Brown with Black Ferns	$5/8$ yard	Cut 7 strips $2^1/2$" wide.
Gold with Dark Gold Flowers	$5/8$ yard	Cut 7 strips $2^1/2$" wide.
Brown with Gold & Green Print	$5/8$ yard	Cut 7 strips $2^1/2$" wide.
Medium Green with Dark Green Fern	$5/8$ yard	Cut 7 strips $2^1/2$" wide.
Green with Cream Floral	$5/8$ yard	Cut 7 strips $2^1/2$" wide.
Dark Green with Light Green Leaves	$5/8$ yard	Cut 7 strips $2^1/2$" wide.
Dark Brown with Beige Dots	$1/2$ yard	Cut 7 strips $1^1/2$" wide for 1st border.
Beige with Green & Black Leaves	$1^1/4$ yards	Cut 7 strips 5" wide for 2nd border.

Dark Red with Cream Floral	$1/4$ yard	Cut 1 strip $5^3/8$" wide, then cut into 2 squares $5^3/8$" x $5^3/8$".
		    Cut each square once on the diagonal to make 4 triangles.
		    Cut the remainder of the strip $2^1/2$" wide, then cut into 4 squares $2^1/2$" x $2^1/2$". Cut the remainder of the strip 2" wide, then cut into 4 squares 2" x 2".

Brown & Cream Check	$5/8$ yard	Cut 8 strips $2^1/4$" wide for binding.
Backing	$3^3/4$ yards	Piece horizontally.

Other materials: thread for appliqué

Press seams in the direction of the arrows unless otherwise indicated.

◆ BLOCK ASSEMBLY

1. Sew together 1 each of the light brown, gold, and brown 2½" strips. Make 7 strip sets. Press. Cut into 6½" segments to make 38 Block A's.

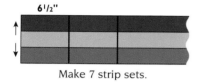

Make 7 strip sets.

Block A Make 38.

2. Sew together 1 each of the medium green, green, and dark green 2½" strips. Make 7 strip sets. Press. Cut into 6½" segments to make 38 Block B's.

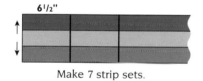

Make 7 strip sets.

Block B Make 38.

3. Draw a diagonal line across 4 Block A's. The strips of Block A will be vertical. Trim 2 of the blocks ¼" to the left of the diagonal and 2 of the blocks ¼" to the right of the diagonal, as shown.

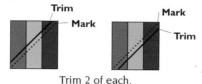

Trim 2 of each.

4. Draw a diagonal line across 4 Block B's. The strips of Block B will be horizontal. Trim 2 of the blocks ¼" to the left of the diagonal and 2 of the blocks ¼" to the right of the diagonal, as shown.

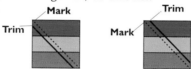

Trim 2 of each.

5. Sew 2 half-Block A's to each of 2 Block B's, as shown, to make 1 each of Unit C and Unit C reversed. Press.

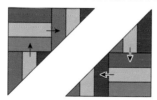

Make 1 of each.

6. Sew 2 half-Block B's to each of 2 Block A's to make 1 each of Unit D and Unit D reversed. Press.

Make 1 of each.

◆ CENTER APPLIQUÉ SQUARE

Refer to Quilting Basics on page 92 for appliqué instructions.

1. Fold the 17½" square of background fabric into quarters; press creases.

2. Using the method of your choice, appliqué 2 dark red with black A doves and 2 medium red A doves to the background square. Place the marked line of each dove on a crease.

3. Sew Units C and D to the center appliqué square. Press.

QUILT ASSEMBLY

1. Sew groups of 8 blocks of A and B together, then sew to the center appliqué unit. Press.

2. Sew the remaining blocks in rows. Press toward Block A.

3. Sew the rows and center appliqué unit together.

First Border

Before cutting all final borders, measure your quilt top to confirm measurements for the strip lengths.

1. Piece dark brown $1^{1}/_{2}$"-wide strips end-to-end as necessary and cut 2 borders to measure $48^{1}/_{2}$" long. Sew to the top and bottom of the quilt. Press.

2. Piece remaining $1^{1}/_{2}$"-wide strips together end-to-end as necessary and cut 2 borders to measure $62^{1}/_{2}$" long. Sew to the sides of the quilt. Press.

Corner Block Assembly

1. Draw a diagonal line across the wrong side of 4 cream $2^{1}/_{2}$" x $2^{1}/_{2}$" squares.

2. Place each marked square, right sides together, on a dark red with cream $2^{1}/_{2}$" x $2^{1}/_{2}$" square. Sew $^{1}/_{4}$" from each side of the diagonal line. Cut in half on the diagonal line, and square up to 2". Press seams open. Make 8 half-square triangle units.

2" Half-Square Triangle Unit
Make 8.

3. Sew a cream triangle to the left side of a half-square triangle unit, and sew a dark red with cream 2" x 2" square to the right side to make Unit A. Press.

4. Sew a cream triangle to the left side and bottom of a half-square triangle to make Unit B. Press.

5. Sew Unit A and B together to make Section 1. Press.

Section 1

6. Sew Section 1 to a dark red with cream $5^{3}/_{8}$" triangle. Piece corner blocks. Press. Make 4.

Make 4.

Second Border

1. Piece beige 5"-wide strips end-to-end as necessary and cut 2 borders to measure $50^{1}/_{2}$" long. Sew to the top and bottom of the quilt. Press.

2. Piece beige 5"-wide strips end-to-end as necessary and cut 2 borders to measure $62^{1}/_{2}$" long.

3. Sew corner blocks to each end of the side borders. Press. Sew to the sides of the quilt. Press.

FINISHING

Refer to Quilting Basics on page 91.

1. Layer the backing, batting, and quilt top; baste.

2. Quilt as desired.

3. Attach a hanging sleeve if desired.

4. Bind or finish as desired.

5. Attach a label.

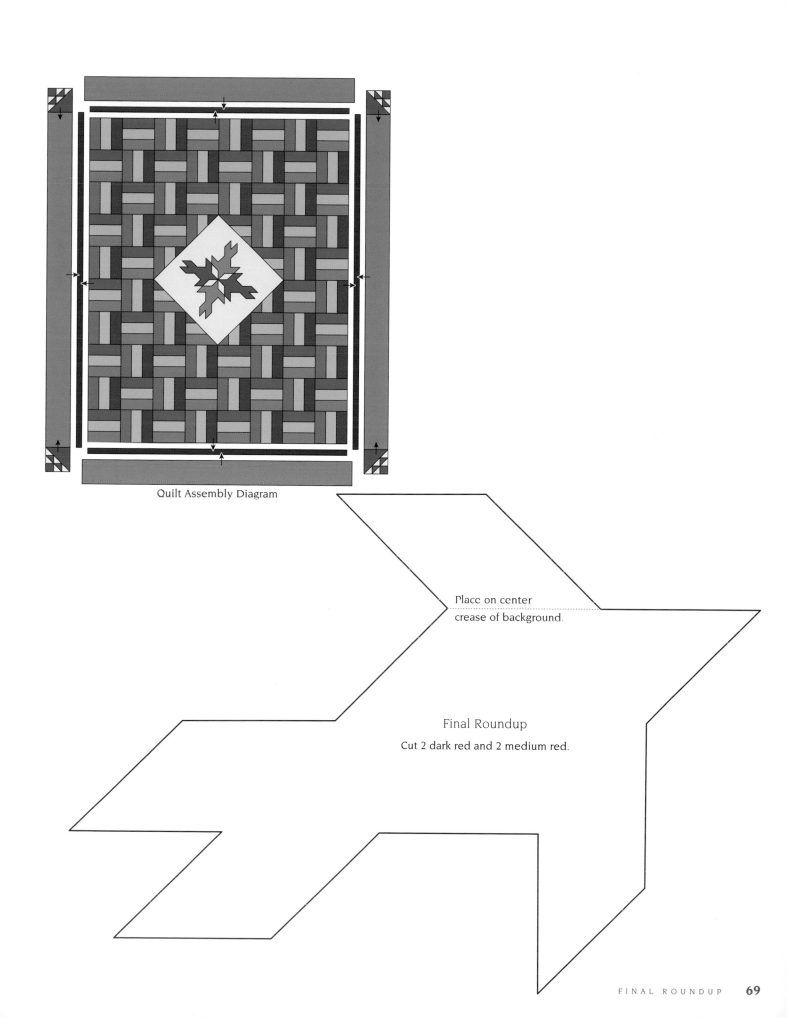

Quilt Assembly Diagram

Place on center
crease of background.

Final Roundup

Cut 2 dark red and 2 medium red.

Coming Storms

"What do you think?" I asked my best friend, Elvia. It was the third outfit I'd tried on, and I was getting desperate. Tonight was my first official date with Gabe Ortiz, a man I'd only known three weeks but had already kissed twice.

"I like the top," she said, critically eyeing my cream-colored silk shirt. "But the navy skirt makes you look like you're ready to argue your client down to a misdemeanor."

I followed her gaze into the long mirror in my bedroom. She was right. The navy wool skirt made me look like an attorney.

"What am I going to wear?" I moaned and sat down hard on the bed. "Maybe I should just cancel. I'm too old to be doing this. I haven't dated since I was a teenager."

"Don't you dare say that," said Elvia, who, at thirty-four, was only a few weeks younger than me. "Quit being such a baby. I go through this all the time. Trust me, he probably won't even notice what you're wearing."

I flopped backward on the bed and stared at the whitewashed ceiling of my rented Spanish bungalow, where I'd lived since my first husband Jack died. "Oh, he'll notice. Gabe's a cop. They notice *everything*."

"He's a *man*," she said, a slight frown wrinkling her perfect black eyebrows. "Wear the silk shirt and a pair of jeans. And put on that tweed blazer I brought. Casual elegance. That's perfect for dinner in Morro Bay."

It started raining lightly an hour before Gabe arrived. Thank goodness the top was up on his sky-blue Corvette. My hair, curly and unruly under the calmest weather conditions, would have become a fright wig had I spent even two minutes in the wind. He was wearing a pair of black jeans, a white shirt, and tweedy blazer. I silently blessed my fashion- and dating-experienced friend. Casual elegance seemed to be the norm when you went out on a first date with someone you'd 1) been investigated by for murder and 2) already shared more than one intimate kiss with.

"You look great," he said when I opened the door. He leaned down to kiss my cheek. The warmth from his lips lingered on my skin for minutes afterward.

"Thanks," I said, wondering if I was supposed to tell him he looked great too. He did, but the words stuck in my throat.

"Do you like seafood?" he asked while we were driving down to Morro Bay, about twelve miles out of San Celina, where we both lived.

"Sure," I said. "As long as it's cooked." I was nixing sushi right from the get-go.

"I wasn't sure, what with you being a rancher and all." His face was expressionless.

Was that a dig at me and my family, ranchers on the central coast for thirty-five years? "I do eat something other than beef once in a while," I said, trying to keep my voice low and noncommittal.

■ Morro Rock can be seen from the deck of the house Benni inherits in *Mariner's Compass.*

■ Seagulls are plentiful in San Luis Obispo County, but so are other birds. Cranes, herons, pelicans, hawks, and even eagles can be seen throughout the county.

■ Harmony is a one-block town on Highway 1 between Cayucos and Cambria. Benni seeks a clue to a mysterious benefactor's identity here in *Mariner's Compass.*

He grinned at me, a brilliantly white smile against his dark skin. "C'mon, I was just teasing you. One of my captains told me about a good restaurant on the Embarcadero called Sam's Fresh Fish. My son's name is Sam, so I thought it might be a good omen." He gave me another devastating smile, and my heart did a quick two-step.

How many awkward situations did that smile get him through? He was just too dang good-looking. Men who had his looks could not be anything but shallow, despite the fact that he hadn't seemed that way. Maybe I'd just been dazzled by his looks, just like every other woman who met him.

"Considering how much grief he sometimes causes me," he continued, "it might not be a good sign."

Was I supposed to ask about his son now? Ask what kind of trouble he gets into? I didn't have kids so I wasn't sure what the protocol was, especially when you were dating.

"He's a basically good kid," Gabe said.

Good, I thought. He doesn't expect an answer.

"He's down at UC Santa Barbara. It's his first year."

"What's his major?" I asked. That had to be a safe topic.

He grinned at me. "Surfing. With a minor in driving his parents crazy."

I laughed and felt a little more comfortable. He sounded like he loved his son. That was always a positive sign.

At the restaurant, when the waiter brought our shrimp cocktails, the gentle rain had turned into an adolescent storm, energetic and unpredictable. Talk about your omens. Although it was Saturday night, a few weeks before Christmas, the restaurant was almost empty. Our table was next to the big picture window.

A powerful wind whistled and wailed outside. We could see the boats in the harbor rocking back and forth, their masts as fragile as toothpicks. A gull gallantly beat his wings, flying against the wind for some unknown reason.

"Wow," Gabe said, spreading his napkin across his lap.

"Yeah," I agreed, picking up my fork, stabbing a pink shrimp, and dipping it into the red cocktail sauce. At that moment, a blast of wind hit the window, startling me. I jumped and the shrimp flew off my fork, hit my chest, and landed in my lap.

I looked down at the red smear across the front of my cream-colored silk shirt. It looked like someone had stabbed me.

"Well, shoot," I said, feeling like the biggest slob on earth. I scrubbed at it with my napkin, making it worse. It wasn't even in a spot that could be covered up by my blazer. I glanced up at him and felt my cheeks turn hot as a branding iron.

He looked at me a moment and took off his jacket. Then, smiling his heart-melting smile, he dipped his finger into his shrimp cocktail and slowly drew a red heart on his own pristine white shirt. His blue-gray eyes, the same color as the swirling ocean outside, never left mine for a moment.

"You have got to be kidding," Elvia said later that night when I called her with a full report. "That doesn't sound like any man I've ever dated. What do you think?"

"Like Yogi Berra says, it's déjà vu all over again," I replied, laughing. I wasn't about to use the words "in love" yet. But I was sure thinking them.

■ The city of Parkfield, "earthquake capital of the world," is actually in southern Monterey County. I use it in *Mariner's Compass* as another place where Benni seeks a clue to the mysterious benefactor.

■ This is part of Port San Luis and Harford pier, outside the town of Avila Beach. In *Irish Chain*, I call them Port San Patricio and Eola Beach. This is the pier Benni falls from in *Irish Chain*. Fat Cat Café, at the base of the pier, is a favorite local hangout.

Coming Storms

Designed by Margrit Hall
Made by Cathryn Tallman-Evans
Quilted by Phyllis Reddish

Finished Block Size: 14"
Finished Quilt Size: 58$\frac{1}{2}$" x 72$\frac{1}{2}$"
Fabric graciously supplied by Robert Kaufman Fabrics.

✳ FABRICS AND CUTTING

Patterns for paper-pieced Mariner's Compass block and corner block are located on the pullout.

FABRIC COLOR	FABRIC AMOUNT	CUTTING DIRECTIONS
Light Blue Background	$2^1/8$ yards	Cut 2 strips $3^3/8$" wide, then cut into 24 squares $3^3/8$" x $3^3/8$". Cut each square once on the diagonal to make 48 triangles. Cut 8 strips 4" wide. Stack strips with wrong sides together and cut 96 pairs of A's (96 A and 96 A reverse). Cut 6 strips $2^1/8$" wide, then cut into 96 squares $2^1/8$" x $2^1/8$". Cut each square once on the diagonal to make 192 triangles. Cut 2 strips 2" wide, then cut into 32 rectangles 2" x $2^1/2$". Set aside for paper-pieced Mariner's Compass corner block. Cut 3 strips 3" wide, then cut into 32 squares 3" x 3". Set aside for paper-pieced Mariner's Compass corner block.
Blue & Green Wave	$1^3/4$ yards	Cut 2 strips 4" wide, then cut into 12 squares 4" x 4". Cut 7 strips $6^1/2$" wide. Set aside for 3rd border.
Dark Blue Swirl	1 yard	Cut 3 strips $4^3/8$" wide, then cut into 24 squares $4^3/8$" x $4^3/8$". Cut each square on the diagonal to make 48 triangles. Cut 6 strips 2" wide. Set aside for 1st border.
Purple Multicolor	$7/8$ yard	Cut 6 strips 4" wide, then cut into 96 B's.
Dark Turquoise	$5/8$ yard	Cut 7 strips $2^5/8$" wide, then cut into 96 squares $2^5/8$" x $2^5/8$". Cut each square once on the diagonal to make 192 triangles.
Light Turquoise	$5/8$ yard	Cut 3 strips $2^1/4$" wide, then cut into 48 squares $2^1/4$" x $2^1/4$". Cut 7 strips $1^1/4$" wide. Set aside for 2nd border.
Dark Purple Solid	$1/2$ yard	Cut 1 strip $2^1/2$" wide, then cut into 4 rectangles 7" x $2^1/2$". Set aside for paper-pieced center Mariner's Compass block. Cut 1 strip 4" wide, then cut into 16 rectangles 4" x $1^1/2$". Set aside for paper-pieced Mariner's Compass corner block.
Light Purple Solid	$1/2$ yard	Cut 1 strip $2^1/2$" wide, then cut into 4 rectangles 7" x $2^1/2$". Set aside for paper-pieced center Mariner's Compass block. Cut 1 strip 4" wide, then cut into 16 rectangles 4" x $1^1/2$". Set aside for paper-pieced Mariner's Compass corner block.
Dark Green Solid	$3/8$ yard	Cut 1 strip 2" wide, then cut into 4 rectangles $5^1/2$" x 2". Set aside for paper-pieced center Mariner's Compass block. Cut 1 strip $3^1/2$" wide, then cut into 16 rectangles $3^1/2$" x 1". Set aside for paper-pieced Mariner's Compass corner block.
Light Green Solid	$3/8$ yard	Cut 1 strip 2" wide, then cut into 4 rectangles $5^1/2$" x 2". Set aside for paper-pieced center Mariner's Compass block. Cut 1 strip $3^1/2$" wide, then cut into 16 rectangles $3^1/2$" x $1^1/4$". Set aside for paper-pieced Mariner's Compass corner block.

Continued next page

FABRIC COLOR	FABRIC AMOUNT	CUTTING DIRECTIONS
Dark Orange Solid	¼ yard	Cut 1 strip 1¼" wide, then cut into 8 rectangles 1¼" x 4½". Set aside for paper-pieced center Mariner's Compass block. Cut 1 strip 2¼" wide, then cut into 32 rectangles 2¼" x 1". Set aside for paper-pieced Mariner's Compass corner block.
Light Orange Solid	¼ yard	Cut 1 strip 1¼" wide, then cut into 8 rectangles 1¼" x 4½". Set aside for paper-pieced center Mariner's Compass block. Cut 1 strip 2¼" wide, then cut into 32 rectangles 2¼" x 1". Set aside for paper-pieced Mariner's Compass corner block.
Dark Teal	⅝ yard	Cut 8 strips 2¼" wide for binding.
Backing	3⅝ yards	Piece horizontally.

Other materials: thread for appliqué

Press seams in the direction of the arrows unless otherwise indicated.

BLOCK ASSEMBLY

1. Sew 3⅜" light blue background triangles to opposite sides of a blue and green 4" x 4" square. Press. Sew 3⅜" background triangles to the remaining sides of the 4" x 4" blue and green square to make Unit A. Press. Make 12 Unit A's.

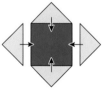

Unit A Make 12.

2. Sew 4⅜" dark blue triangles to opposite sides of Unit A. Press. Sew 4⅜" dark blue triangles to the remaining sides of Unit A to make Section 1. Press. Make 12 Section 1's.

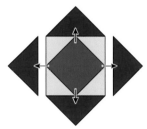

Section 1 Make 12.

3. Sew a background A triangle to the right side and a background A reverse triangle to the left side of a purple B triangle to make Unit B. Press. Make 96 Unit B's.

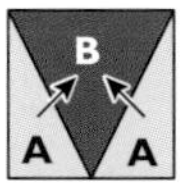

Unit B Make 96.

4. Sew 2 Unit B's together to make Section 2. Press. Make 48 Section 2's.

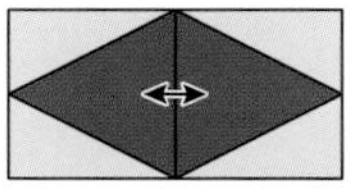

Section 2 Make 48.

■ Margrit used this photo of the ocean to inspire the quilt *Coming Storms*. Her husband, David, took it when they were up on the central coast doing research.

■ A daytime view of Morro Rock, which figures prominently in the book *Mariner's Compass*.

■ Another view of the San Luis Obispo County Historical Museum. This is one of the few places in my fictional town of San Celina that looks exactly like the real place on which I based it.

■ James Dean was killed in SLO County near Cholame. A monument was placed here by a dedicated fan. At the café next to it, Benni finds another clue on the scavenger hunt she goes on in *Mariner's Compass*.

5. Sew 2⅛" background triangles to opposite sides of a light turquoise 2¼" x 2¼" square. Press. Sew 2⅛" background triangles to the remaining sides of the square to make Unit C. Press. Make 48 Unit C's.

Unit C Make 48.

6. Sew 2⅝" dark turquoise triangles to opposite sides of Unit C. Press. Sew 2⅝" dark turquoise triangles to the remaining sides of Unit C to make Section 3. Make 48 Section 3's.

Section 3 Make 48.

7. Sew the sections together to make a complete block. Press seams open. Make 12 blocks.

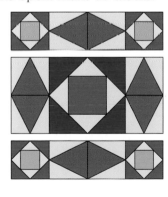

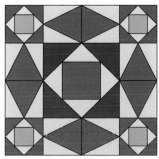

Complete Block Make 12.

QUILT ASSEMBLY

1. Sew 3 blocks together for each row. Press seams open.

2. Sew the rows together to make the quilt body. Press seams open.

First Border

Before cutting all final borders, measure your quilt top to confirm measurements for the strip lengths.

1. Sew 2"-wide dark blue strips end-to-end as necessary and cut 2 border strips 42½" long. Sew to the top and bottom of the quilt and press.

2. Sew 2"-wide dark blue strips end-to-end as necessary and cut 2 border strips 59½" long. Sew to the sides of the quilt and press.

Second Border

1. Sew 1¼"-wide light turquoise strips end-to-end as necessary and cut 2 border strips 45½" long. Sew to the top and bottom of the quilt and press.

2. Sew 1¼"-wide light turquoise strips end-to-end as necessary and cut 2 border strips 61" long. Sew to the sides of the quilt and press.

Corner Block Assembly

Refer to Quilting Basics on page 93 for paper-piecing instructions.

1. Using the precut rectangles and squares (See pullout), paper-piece Section A and Section B of the corner blocks. Make 16 of each section.

Section A Make 16.

Section B Make 16.

2. Sew a Section A to a Section B to make one-quarter of the corner block. Press seam open. Make 8.

One-Quarter Block Make 8.

3. Sew quarters into halves, and then sew 2 halves together to make a corner block. Make 4 corner blocks. Trim to a 6½" x 6½" square. Press seam open. Remove the paper.

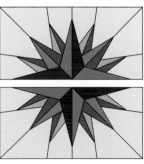

Make 4 corner blocks.

Third Border

1. Sew 6$\frac{1}{2}$"-wide blue and green strips end-to-end as necessary and cut 2 border strips 47" long. Sew to the top and bottom of the quilt and press.

2. Sew 6$\frac{1}{2}$"-wide blue and green strips end-to-end as necessary and cut 2 border strips 61" long.

3. Sew corner blocks to both ends of each side strip. Press. Sew to the sides of the quilt and press.

Center Mariner's Compass Appliqué

See Quilting Basics on page 93 for paper-piecing instructions.

1. Using the precut rectangles and squares, paper-piece Sections A and B of the center Mariner's Compass block. Sew to the dots and backstitch. Do not sew through the $\frac{1}{4}$" seam allowance. Make 4 of each section.

2. Sew A and B together to make one-quarter of the block. Sew to the dots and backstitch. Do not sew through the $\frac{1}{4}$" seam allowance.

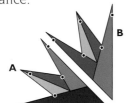

One-quarter of the block Make 4.

3. Sew quarters into halves, and then sew 2 halves together to make the block. Sew to the dots and backstitch. Do not sew through the $\frac{1}{4}$" seam allowance. Trim and remove the paper.

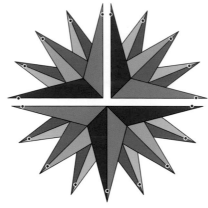

Completing the Mariner's Compass Block

4. Mark and turn under $\frac{1}{4}$" seam allowances around the edges of the block. Press edges under and appliqué to the quilt. Use the quilt photo on page 72 for placement.

▓ FINISHING

Refer to Quilting Basics on page 91.

1. Layer the backing, batting, and quilt top; baste.

2. Quilt as desired.

3. Attach a hanging sleeve if desired.

4. Bind or finish as desired.

5. Attach a label.

Quilt Assembly Diagram

A Mother's Love

9 "I found this in an old trunk," Daddy said to me. He handed me a letter, faded to a pale, creamy yellow. The front of it just said "Mother." I recognized the slanted, elegant script of my own mother, who died when I was six.

"Did you read it?" I asked, turning the thin envelope over and over in my hands.

He nodded but didn't speak. For the first time in my thirty-five years, I saw tears well up in my stoic father's eyes. He looked down briefly and settled his brown Stetson on his head with one work-scarred hand. "I think she'd want you to have it."

I watched him walk away, his fifty-six-year-old shoulders stooped slightly. Although I never thought of my father as being old, I suddenly realized that he'd been widowed for twenty-nine years. That was a long time to be alone. Why hadn't he ever remarried or even dated? I'd never asked him, and he'd never told me. Not unusual for a man who may have been born in Arkansas but who had taken to the silent Western male persona as if he'd been born to it.

I had been widowed for only eleven months and was now dating someone, our town's impossibly handsome and sometimes frustrating police chief, Gabriel Ortiz. Even his name could make my heart beat a little faster. Was I in love? It sure felt like it, though he was as different from my first husband, Jack, my childhood sweetheart, as a person could be. But I felt the same adolescent thrill when I saw Gabe that I used to feel when Jack drove up to our ranch in his old army Jeep.

I sat down on the front porch swing and gazed out at the oak tree that still held the tire swing Daddy made for me when I was five. He told me my mother used to watch me swing on it while she sat up on this very porch, too weak from cancer to push me herself. I don't remember her on the porch. Or much about her at all.

I held the envelope up to my nose, hoping for a hint of her scent. All I smelled was the faint odor of cedar. This had probably been kept in the cedar chest that sat at the foot of Daddy's bed for as long as I could remember.

■ Here's a pair of my wilder red boots. (Benni's cousin, Rita, would probably steal these boots from me.)

■ I have no idea what possessed me when I bought these cowboy boots, but I love them! They are not something Benni would buy.

■ This is the last photo I had taken with my maternal grandmother Webb, who was born in Arkansas. She was the quilter in the family, who thought I was nuts when I hung the quilts she made on my walls.

■ Me and a friend's colt. People often ask me if I have horses, and I always say, "No, I have something better. I have friends who have horses!"

April 12, 1958
Sugartree, Arkansas

Dear Mama,

I wish you were here to see your granddaughter. She was born with your reddish-blonde curls! And my and Daddy's stubbornness, I fear. Though she is almost three weeks old, she is already a woman who knows her own mind. She has definite likes and dislikes, something I find amazing. How can a baby this young make choices? If you were here, maybe you could explain that to me, maybe even tell me what I was like at this age. Did I prefer absolute quiet in my room at night or a little bit of music from the radio? Did new people make me cry or gurgle with pleasure? Did I like being rocked or sang to? Oh, how I wish you were here to answer these questions. I know at twenty I am considered to be an adult, somebody's mother! That is just amazing to me because what I need most right now is a mother myself. My dear mother-in-law, Dove, is a wonderful help and comfort to me and she answers all my questions, but only you could tell me how it felt to be a mother to me, how I appeared at this age. Oh, Mama, you were taken too young. You never got to see your first grandchild. I know God has a plan for all of us, but I cannot help wishing that His plan had included you being with me a little longer.

I must put down my pen now. Benni is awake and hungry, something she doesn't mind a bit telling the world about! Ben is enamored, of course, and is already talking about buying her first pony. I told him let's concentrate on teaching her to sit up first. I do love my dear husband. And I love you, Mama, and look forward to the time when we will see each other again.

Your loving daughter, Alice

P.S. Can you see the beautiful signature quilt my Sunday School friends made for Benni? It is just gorgeous. You'd love this little church we are attending. The preacher reminds me of Daddy a little, very boisterous and cheerful. He makes us stand and sit so often during the service that some of the people are complaining he's half Catholic! It's wicked of me to say, but some of the people can really use the exercise! Bless our hearts, we Baptists do love to complain, don't we?

■ Here's a pair of my conservative red boots (I have four pairs).

■ I've helped many of my ranching friends with their cattle chores. This is a bull calf owned by my friend, Joy Fitzhugh. She named him "Brat" for a very good reason!

A Mother's Love

Designed by Margrit Hall

Made by Robyn Malone

Quilted by Ginny Jaranowski

Finished Block Size: 8"

Finished Quilt Size: 42½" x 42½"

Fabrics graciously supplied by RJR Fabrics.

❤ FABRICS AND CUTTING

Heart and embroidery patterns are located on the pullout.

FABRIC COLOR	FABRIC AMOUNT	CUTTING DIRECTIONS
Background	2¹/₂ yards	Cut 6 strips 4¹/₂" wide, then cut into 14 squares 4¹/₂" x 4¹/₂" for stars and 2nd border and 64 rectangles 4¹/₂" x 2¹/₂" for stars. Cut 13 strips 2¹/₂" wide, then cut into 64 squares 2¹/₂" x 2¹/₂" for stars and 136 squares 2¹/₂" x 2¹/₂" for 2nd border. Cut 5 strips 2¹/₄" wide for binding.
Pink 1	³/₈ yard	Cut 1 strip 4¹/₂" wide, then cut into 2 squares 4¹/₂" x 4¹/₂" for stars and 10 rectangles 4¹/₂" x 2¹/₂" for 2nd border. Cut 1 strip 2¹/₂" wide, then cut into 16 squares 2¹/₂" x 2¹/₂" for stars.
Pinks 2, 3, and 4	³/₈ yard **each**	From each fabric, cut 1 strip 2¹/₂" wide, then cut into 16 squares 2¹/₂" x 2¹/₂". Cut 1 strip 4¹/₂" wide, then cut into 8 rectangles 4¹/₂" x 2¹/₂" for 2nd border.
Blue 1	³/₈ yard	Cut 1 strip 4¹/₂" wide, then cut 2 squares 4¹/₂" x 4¹/₂" for stars and 10 rectangles 4¹/₂" x 2¹/₂" for 2nd border. Cut 1 strip 2¹/₂" wide, then cut into 16 squares 2¹/₂" x 2¹/₂" for stars.
Blue 2	¹/₂ yard	Cut 1 strip 4¹/₂" wide, then cut into 2 squares 4¹/₂" x 4¹/₂" for stars and 8 rectangles 4¹/₂" x 2¹/₂" for 2nd border. Cut 1 strip 2¹/₂" wide, then cut into 16 squares 2¹/₂" x 2¹/₂" for stars.
Blues 3 & 4	³/₈ yard **each**	From each fabric, cut 1 strip 2¹/₂" wide, then cut into 16 squares 2¹/₂" x 2¹/₂" for stars. Cut 1 strip 4¹/₂" wide, then cut into 8 rectangles 4¹/₂" x 2¹/₂" for 2nd border.
Blue 5	¹/₄ yard	Cut 4 strips 1¹/₂" wide for 1st border.
Backing	2 ³/₄ yards	Piece together.

Other materials: embroidery floss

❤ BLOCK EMBROIDERY

1. Using a pencil, lightly trace the embroidery pattern onto 10 background 4¹/₂" x 4¹/₂" squares. Refer to the quilt photo on page 79 for suggested placement. You may choose to reverse the designs on some of the squares or vary the number of flowers in the design.

2. Embroider the designs using 3 strands of embroidery floss. Embroider the stems with a stem stitch. Embroider the leaves and flowers with a lazy daisy stitch. Make a French knot at the center of each flower.

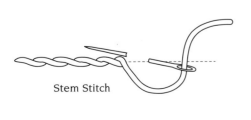

Stem Stitch

Lazy Daisy Stitch

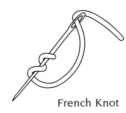

French Knot

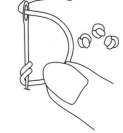

3. Embroider quotes of your choice or write them using a very fine-point permanent marker. You may choose to personalize the quilt by having friends and family sign the blocks.

When this you see, remember me —Ida Pendleton

Welcome, little one —Rose Mae Lovelis

Love to the little one —Glessie Wilcox

Bless you and the little baby —June Willows

Train up a child in the way he should go–Proverbs 22:6
—Carlene Kelligrew

As the twig is bent, so grows the child–Congratulations
—Judy Renault

Happiness always —Caroline Maplegrove

Love from your sister-in-heart —Gwen Swanson

Friendship is a sheltering tree —Agnes Bickles

Hands to work, hearts to God —Elizabeth Clark

Excerpts from *Mariner's Compass,* page 159

Note: Press all seams in the direction of the arrows, unless otherwise indicated.

❤ BLOCK ASSEMBLY

1. Draw a diagonal line across the wrong side of each pink or blue $2\frac{1}{2}$" x $2\frac{1}{2}$" square.

2. Place a marked square on a $4\frac{1}{2}$" x $2\frac{1}{2}$" background rectangle with right sides together.

3. Sew on the diagonal and trim $\frac{1}{4}$" from the sewing line. Press.

4. Repeat on the opposite end of the rectangle to make Unit A. Make 4 Unit A's for each star (64 total).

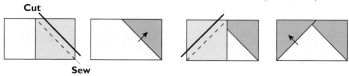

Unit A Make 4 for each star.

5. Sew a $2\frac{1}{2}$" x $2\frac{1}{2}$" square of background fabric to each side of Unit A to make Unit B. Press. Make 2 Unit B's for each star (32 total).

Unit B Make 2 for each star.

6. Sew a Unit A to each side of a $4\frac{1}{2}$" x $4\frac{1}{2}$" star center square of the matching color to make Unit C. Press.

7. Sew Unit B's to the top and bottom of Unit C to make a block. Make 2 blocks each using Pink Fabric 1, Blue Fabric 1, and Blue Fabric 2 (6 blocks total).

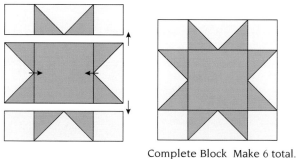

Complete Block Make 6 total.

8. Repeat using remaining Unit A's and B's and a $4\frac{1}{2}$" background embroidered signature square block for each star center. Make 2 blocks with each fabric, 6 total.

♥ QUILT ASSEMBLY

1. Referring to the quilt photo on page 79 and the Quilt Assembly Diagram, arrange the blocks. Sew the blocks into rows. Press seams of alternating rows in opposite directions.

2. Sew rows together and press.

First Borders

Before cutting all final borders, measure your quilt top to confirm measurements for the strip lengths.

1. Cut 2 Blue Fabric 5 strips $1^{1}/_{2}$" wide to measure $32^{1}/_{2}$" long and sew to the top and bottom of the quilt. Press.

2. Cut the remaining Blue Fabric 5 strips to measure $34^{1}/_{2}$" long and sew to the sides the quilt. Press.

Second Border

1. Draw a diagonal line across the wrong side of each remaining background $2^{1}/_{2}$" x $2^{1}/_{2}$" square.

2. Place a marked square on a $4^{1}/_{2}$" x $2^{1}/_{2}$" colored rectangle with right sides together.

3. Sew, cut, and press, following Steps 1–4 on page 81, to make the flying geese units for the 2nd border. Make 10 each of Pink Fabric 1 and Blue Fabric 1 and 8 each of Pink Fabrics 2–4 and Blue Fabrics 2–4 (68 total).

Flying Geese Border Unit Make 68 total.

4. Referring to the quilt photo and assembly diagram, sew flying geese units together into 4 border strips of 17 units each. Press.

5. Sew 2 border strips to the top and bottom of the quilt. Press.

6. Using the method of your choice, appliqué a heart in the center of each of the 4 background fabric $4^{1}/_{2}$" x $4^{1}/_{2}$" squares.

7. Embroider around each heart using a buttonhole stitch.

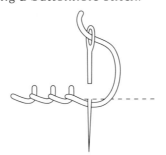

Buttonhole Stitch

8. Sew an appliquéd heart square to each end of the 2 side border strips and press. Sew to the sides of the quilt. Press.

♥ FINISHING

Refer to Quilting Basics on page 91.

1. Layer the backing, batting, and quilt top; baste.

2. Quilt as desired.

3. Attach a hanging sleeve if desired.

4. Bind or finish as desired.

5. Attach a label.

Quilt Assembly Diagram

She Shall Overcome

9 "Let me read you what I have so far," Emory said. "We really need to finish this interview today so I can turn it in to the newspaper. They're going to run it on the front page."

"I need to feed my chickens," Dove replied. "Read to me while we walk."

Emory followed the woman he and everyone else called Dove out the back door toward the chicken coop in the back pasture. Born and raised in Arkansas, just like him, Dove was related to his mother in some complex, Southern way that he could never quite get straight. He'd always just thought of her as his gramma Dove. She and his cousin, Benni, were the two women he loved and trusted most in this world. They'd both been there for him when he was a frightened, eleven-year-old boy whose mother had died and whose father went temporarily crazy from grief. Twenty-four years ago, that scary, childhood summer he spent here at the Ramsey ranch on the central coast of California saved his life and profoundly affected how he viewed women.

"Okay, this is what I've written," he said.

San Celina Profiles
This Dove Hits Her Mark Every Time
by Emory Littleton

She can field dress a deer, deliver a new calf, shoot a .45 pistol at a man-shaped target and not once miss her preferred mark (don't ask), raise six children and one granddaughter, stitch innumerable quilts, and bake a strawberry angel food cake that would bring an honest man to his knees.

She has also managed, in her spare time, to save our local historical museum from being sold to a steakhouse chain. She and her fellow protestors took over the old Carnegie Library and held it physically hostage until our illustrious mayor and city council saw the error of their ways and granted Mrs. Ramsey and her six fellow San Celina Historical Society members a 20-year lease on the building. Nicknamed "The San Celina Seven," they give courage to groups small and large who hope to change an increasingly uncaring system.

"We did what every good citizen should do when they see an injustice," Mrs. Ramsey said. "We acted. We'd tried writing letters and going to meetings but all we heard was yak, yak, yak. So we decided to use our constitutional right to bear arms."

Emory stopped reading and laughed. "You didn't actually have any guns in there, did you?"

"For Heaven's sakes, no," Dove said.

"Well, I quoted you exactly, but I think we should change that. How about you decided to use your Constitutional right to free speech and free assembly?"

"That doesn't sound like something I'd say," she commented, dipping an old can into a barrel of chicken feed.

"Okay, then tell me again. Why did you take over the library?"

"Because those poopheads on the city council and Mayor Poophead himself were going to sell it to a taco chain or something so they'd have more money to spend on fat cat lunches and fancy cars."

"It actually was an upscale steakhouse."

"Whatever." She sprinkled some feed on the ground, and her Rhode Island reds came running.

He chuckled. "You sound like a teenager."

"Can we get on with this? I thought you had a deadline. I need to get back inside and make some pies for the Cattlewomen's Bake Sale this Saturday."

"Okay, let me read you the rest of what I've written."

"My husband fought in World War II and my own grandson-in-law, Gabriel Ortiz, who also happens to be the police chief, is a Vietnam veteran. They risked their lives so we could have the freedom to say what we think and fight for the things we believe in. What they did was a part of our history, and history is exactly what we're trying to preserve in the Historical Museum. The mayor wanted us to pack all the things we'd cataloged and restored in a warehouse somewhere and we weren't about to let that happen. History needs to be out there where kids can see and touch it, so maybe there won't be a World War II or a Vietnam War again."

Mrs. Ramsey is the grandmother of a local woman, Benni Harper, who is curator of the Josiah Sinclair Folk Art Museum and recently married to San Celina's new police chief, Gabriel Ortiz. When asked what she thought of her grandmother's activities, she replied, "All I can say is you don't ever want to get in the way when my gramma sets her mind to something. Those politicians didn't stand a chance. No one kicks patooty like Dove. I think she should run for mayor."

"She said that?" Dove said, an obviously pleased expression on her face. Her white braid flicked back and forth as she sprinkled feed for the fifty or so chickens. "Mayor Ramsey. Has a nice ring to it."

Emory threw back his head and laughed. "Oh, my, that would strike terror in the hearts of many a council member. Not to mention Gabe."

"Oh, pshaw," she said. "I'd let him run the police station any way he likes. He's a good boy."

"Okay, let me read the rest of it to you real quick, and you tell me if there are any inaccuracies."

By the time he was finished reading, she'd thrown the last of the feed out and told the chickens, "That's it, ladies. Café Ramsey is closed until tomorrow."

"I need a punchy ending," Emory said. "Maybe something to do with food, tie that in with politics somehow. What's your favorite food?"

"Anything I don't have to cook."

He thought for a moment. "That's cute, but I don't know . . ."

She looked up from her five-foot nothing and gave him a mischievous smile. "Okay, then, prairie oysters. Sliced thin, breaded, and fried. My absolute favorite dish. Never get tired of 'em. Tell the mayor he'd better not ever forget it either."

"Perfect," Emory said. "Absolutely perfect."

■ The California Poppy is our state flower and can be seen everywhere in the county. Its bright orange-gold color has inspired many local artists.

■ San Luis Obispo County is known for its variety and abundance of produce and wines as well as gourmet restaurants and good, down-home cafes.

■ Carrots at the Farmers' Market

She Shall Overcome

Designed by Margrit Hall
Made by Cathryn Tallman-Evans
Quilted by Kathleen Pappas

Finished Block Size: 12"
Finished Quilt Size: 49" x 49"
Fabric graciously supplied by Robert Kaufman Fabrics Co.

✳ FABRICS AND CUTTING

Template patterns are located on page 89.

FABRIC COLOR	FABRIC AMOUNT	CUTTING DIRECTIONS
White	1⁵/₈ yards	Cut 9 strips 3¹/₂" wide. Set 1 strip aside for Block B. Cut remaining strips into 52 rectangles 3¹/₂" x 2" for Block A and Block B, 20 A's and 20 A reverses for Block A, and 36 B's for Block A and Block B. (See hint below.) Cut 10 strips 2" wide. Set 4 strips aside for Block A and Block B. Cut the remaining strips into 8 strips 2" x 11" and 4 strips 2" x 9¹/₂" for 1st border and 16 squares 2" x 2" and 16 D's for 3rd border corner blocks.
Dark Red	⁵/₈ yard	Cut 1 strip 3¹/₂" wide, then cut into 4 squares 3¹/₂" x 3¹/₂" for Block B. Cut the remainder of the strip 2" wide and cut into 4 squares 2" x 2" for 3rd border corner blocks. Cut 6 strips 2¹/₄" wide for binding.
Medium Red	³/₈ yard	Cut 2 strips 3¹/₂" wide, then cut into 16 A's and 16 A reverses for Block B.
Dark Blue	¹/₄ yard	Cut 1 strip 3¹/₂" wide, then cut into 5 squares 3¹/₂" x 3¹/₂".
Medium Blue	³/₈ yard	Cut 2 strips 3¹/₂" wide, then cut into 20 A's and 20 A reverses for Block A.
Light Blue	³/₈ yard	Cut 2 strips 3¹/₂" wide, then cut into 20 A's and 20 A reverses for Block A.
Red Metallic	³/₈ yard	Cut 5 strips 2" wide. Set 2 strips aside for Block A. Cut 1 of the remaining strips in half to make 2 strips 2" x 20". Set 1 half strip aside for 1st border. Cut the remaining strips into 20 squares 2" x 2" for Block A and 4 squares 2" x 2" for 1st border corner squares and 16 C's and 16 C reverses for 3rd border corner blocks.
Blue Metallic	³/₈ yard	Cut 4 strips 2" wide. Cut 1 strip in half to make 2 strips 2" x 20". Set 1 half-strip and 1 full strip aside for 1st border, and set the remaining 2 strips aside for Block B.
Navy Blue	¹/₄ yard	Cut 4 strips 1" wide for 2nd border.
Navy Blue Fireworks	³/₄ yard	Cut 4 strips 5" wide for 3rd border.
Backing	3 yards	Piece together.

Hint

For A, place 2 strips 3¹/₂" wide wrong sides together. Cut A and A reverse (each cut will make 1 A and 1 A reverse).

Place pattern B on fabric strip and cut.

Press seams in the direction of the arrows, unless otherwise indicated.

🔷 BLOCK A ASSEMBLY

1. Sew a red metallic 2"-wide strip to a white 2"-wide strip. Press. Make 2 red/white strip sets and cut into 40 segments 2" wide.

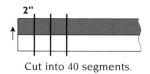

Cut into 40 segments.

2. Sew 2 of the segments together to form a four-patch unit (Unit 1). Press. Make 20.

Unit 1 Make 20.

3. Sew a light blue A triangle to a white A triangle to make Unit 2. Press. Sew a light blue A reverse to a white A reverse to make Unit 2R. Press. Make 20 Unit 2's and 20 Unit 2 reverses.

Unit 2 Make 20. Unit 2R Make 20.

4. Sew a Unit 2 to the left side of a 2" red metallic square to make Unit 3. Press. Sew a Unit 2 reverse to the right side of a 2" red metallic square to make Unit 3R. Press. Make 10 Unit 3's and 10 Unit 3 reverses.

Unit 3 Make 10. Unit 3R Make 10.

5. Sew a medium blue A triangle and a medium blue A reverse triangle to the sides of a white B triangle. Press. Sew a 2" x 3½" white rectangle to the top of the white B triangle and press to make Unit 4. Make 20.

Unit 4 Make 20.

6. Sew units together to make Section 1. Press. Make 10 Section 1's.

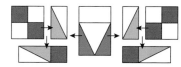

Section 1 Make 10.

7. Sew Unit 4's to either side of a dark blue 3½" x 3½" square to make Section 2. Make 5.

Section 2 Make 5.

8. Sew Section 1's to each side of Section 2 to make Block A. Press. Make 5.

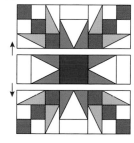

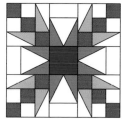

Block A Make 5.

🔷 BLOCK B ASSEMBLY

1. Sew a blue metallic 2"-wide strip to a white 2"-wide strip. Press. Make 2 blue/white strip sets and cut into 32 segments 2" wide. Sew 2 of the segments together to form a four-patch unit (Unit 1). Make 16.

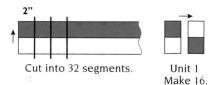

Cut into 32 segments. Unit 1 Make 16.

2. Sew a white 3½"-wide strip to a blue metallic 2"-wide strip to make a strip set. Press and cut into 16 segments 2" wide to make Unit 2.

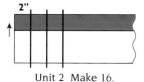

Unit 2 Make 16.

3. Sew a medium red A triangle and a medium red A reverse triangle to the sides of a white B triangle. Press and sew a 2" x 3½" white rectangle to the top of the white B triangle to make Unit 3. Press. Make 16.

Unit 3 Make 16.

4. Sew units and 2" x 3½" white rectangles together to make Section 1. Press. Make 8.

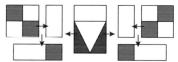

Section 1 Make 8.

5. Sew Unit 4's to each side of a dark red 3½" x 3½" square to make Section 2. Press. Make 4.

Section 2 Make 4.

6. Sew Section 1's to each side of a Section 2 to make Block B. Press. Make 4.

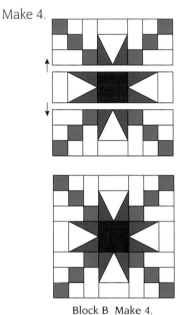

Block B Make 4.

❋ QUILT ASSEMBLY

1. Sew blocks together into rows, alternating A and B blocks. Press seams of alternate rows in opposite directions.

2. Sew the rows together and press.

First Border

Before cutting final borders, measure your quilt top to confirm measurements for the strip lengths.

1. Sew a red metallic 2" x 20" strip to a blue metallic 2" x 20" strip to make a strip set. Press and cut into 8 segments 2" wide.

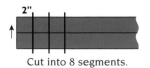

Cut into 8 segments.

2. Sew red/blue metallic segments between 2" x 11" white rectangles and a 2" x 9½" white rectangle. Sew 4 pieced border strips together as shown. Press. Make 4.

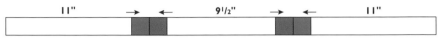

Pieced Border Strips Make 4.

3. Sew 2 of the pieced border strips to the top and bottom of the quilt. Press.

4. Sew a 2" red metallic square to both ends of the remaining pieced border strips. Press and sew to the sides of the quilt. Press.

Second Border

1. Cut 2 of the navy blue strips 1" wide to measure 39½" long. Sew to the top and bottom of the quilt. Press.

2. Cut the remaining navy blue strips 1" wide to measure 40½" long and sew to the sides of the quilt. Press.

Corner Block Assembly

1. Sew a red metallic C triangle and a red metallic C reverse triangle to 2 sides of a white D triangle to make Unit A. Press. Make 16.

Unit A Make 16.

2. Sew 2" x 2" white squares to the sides of Unit A to make Section 1. Press. Make 8.

Section 1 Make 8.

3. Sew Unit A's to the sides of a 2" x 2" dark red square to make Section 2. Press. Make 4.

Section 2 Make 4.

4. Sew Section 1's to each side of a Section 2 to make the corner block. Press. Make 4.

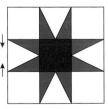

Corner Block Make 4.

Third Border

1. Cut the 4 navy blue fireworks strips 5" wide to measure 40$\frac{1}{2}$" long. Sew 2 of the border strips to the top and bottom of the quilt. Press.

2. Sew corner blocks to both ends of the remaining 40$\frac{1}{2}$"-long border strips and sew to the sides of the quilt. Press.

✦ FINISHING

Refer to Quilting Basics on page 91.

1. Layer the backing, batting, and quilt top; baste.

2. Quilt as desired.

3. Attach a hanging sleeve if desired.

4. Bind or finish as desired.

5. Attach a label.

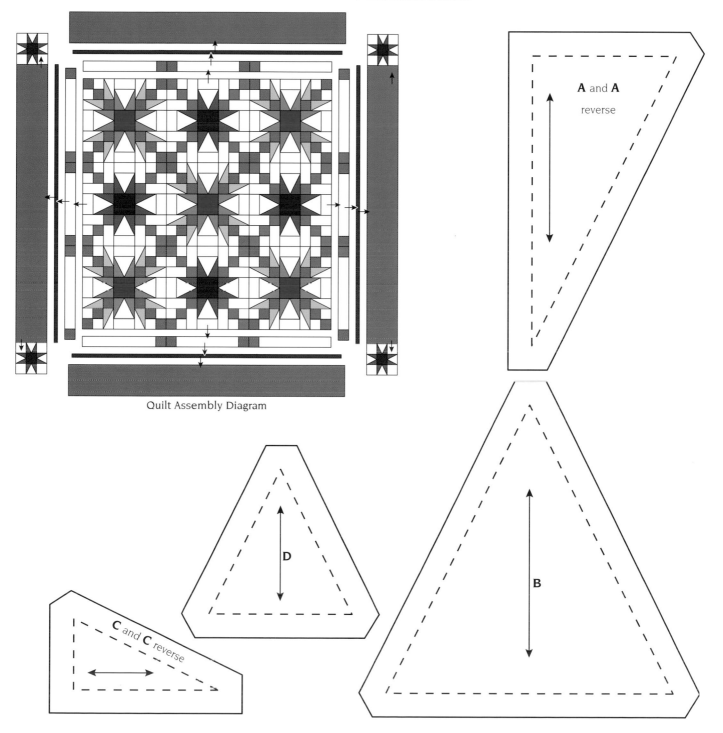

Quilt Assembly Diagram

Quilting Basics

Fabric requirements are based on a 42" width; many fabrics shrink when washed, and widths vary by manufacturer. In cutting instructions, strips are cut on the crosswise grain, unless otherwise indicated.

SEAM ALLOWANCES

A $1/4$" seam allowance is used for most projects. It's a good idea to do a test seam before you begin sewing to check that your $1/4$" is accurate.

PRESSING

In general, press seams toward the darker fabric. Press lightly in an up-and-down motion. Avoid using a very hot iron or over-ironing, which can distort shapes and blocks.

Butted Borders

In most cases, sew the top and bottom borders on first. When you have finished the quilt top, measure it across the center horizontally. This measurement will equal the length for the top and bottom borders. Place pins at the centers of all four sides of the quilt top, as well as in the center of each top and bottom border strip. Pin the top and bottom borders to the quilt top first, matching the center pins. Using a $1/4$" seam allowance, sew the borders to the quilt top and press.

Measure vertically through the center of the quilt top, including the top and bottom borders. This measurement will be the length to cut the side borders. Repeat pinning, sewing, and pressing.

Mitered Corner Borders

Measure the length of the quilt top and add 2 times the width of your border, plus 5". This is the length you need to cut or piece the side for the borders.

Place pins at the centers of both side borders and all four sides of the quilt top. From the center pin, measure in both directions, and mark half of the measured length of the quilt top on both side borders. Pin, matching the centers and the marked length of the side border to the edges of the quilt top. Stitch the strips to the sides of the quilt top.

Stop and backstitch at the seam allowance line, $1/4$" from the edge. The excess length will extend beyond each edge. Press seams toward border.

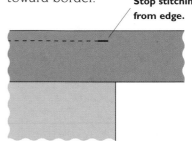

Stop stitching $1/4$" from edge.

Determine the length needed for the top and bottom border the same way, measuring the width of the quilt top through the center and including each side border. Add 5" to this measurement. Cut or piece those border strips. From the center of each border strip, measure in both directions, and mark half of the measured width of the quilt top. Again, pin, stitch up to the $1/4$" seamline, and backstitch. The border strips extend beyond each end.

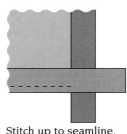

Stitch up to seamline.

To create the miter, lay the corner on the ironing board. Working with the quilt right side up, lay one strip on top of the adjacent border. Fold the top border strip under itself so that it meets the edge of the outer border and forms a 45° angle. Press and pin the fold in place.

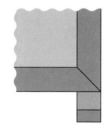

Fold under at a 45° angle.

Position a 90° angle triangle or ruler over the corner to check that the corner is flat and square. When everything is in place, press the fold firmly.

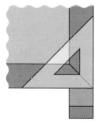

Square corner.

Fold the center section of the top diagonally from the corner, right sides together, and align the long edges of the border strips. On the wrong side, place pins near the pressed fold in the corner to secure the border strips.

Beginning at the inside corner, backstitch and stitch along the fold toward the outside point, being careful not to allow any stretching to occur. Backstitch at the end. Trim the excess border fabric to the ¼" seam allowance. Press the seam open.

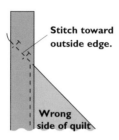

Stitch toward outside edge.

Wrong side of quilt

BACKING

Plan on making the backing a minimum of 2" larger than the quilt top on all sides. Prewash the fabric, and trim the selvages before you piece.

To economize, you may choose to piece the back from any leftover fabrics or blocks in your collection.

BATTING

The type of batting to use is a personal decision; consult your local quilt shop. Cut batting approximately 2" larger on all sides than your quilt top.

LAYERING

Spread the backing wrong side up and tape the edges down with masking tape. (If you are working on carpet, you can use T-pins to secure the backing to the carpet.) Center the batting on top, smoothing out any folds. Place the quilt top right side up on top of the batting and backing, making sure that it is centered.

BASTING

If you plan to machine quilt, pin baste the quilt layers together with safety pins placed a minimum of 3"–4" apart. Begin basting in the center and move toward the edges first in vertical, then horizontal, rows.

If you plan to hand quilt, baste the layers together with thread using a long needle and light-colored thread. Knot one end of the thread. Using stitches approximately the length of the needle, begin in the center and move out toward the edges.

QUILTING

Quilting, whether by hand or machine, enhances the pieced or appliqué design of the quilt. You may choose to quilt in-the-ditch, echo the pieced or appliqué motifs, use patterns from quilting design books and stencils, or do your own free-motion quilting.

DOUBLE-FOLD STRAIGHT-GRAIN BINDING

Trim the excess batting and backing from the quilt. For 1/4" finished binding, cut 2 1/4"-wide strips the width of the fabric. Sew strips together using diagonal seams. Place strips right sides together with ends at right angles. Draw a line from A to B. Sew on the marked line, and trim to the 1/4" seam allowance. Press seam open.

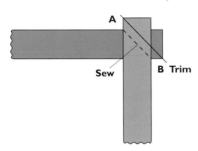

Continue sewing strips together to make a continuous binding strip that will go around the perimeter of the quilt. Fold the strips in half, wrong sides together, and press the entire length of the strip.

Place the raw edges of the quilt and binding together. Pin the binding to one side of the quilt, starting at least 6" from the corner. Making sure to leave the first 3"–4" of binding unattached, sew the binding to the quilt using a 1/4" seam allowance. Stop sewing 1/4" from the corner and backstitch.

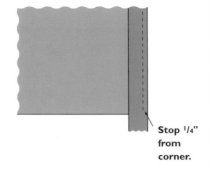

Fold the binding strip at a right angle so that it is extended upward and even with the 2nd side of the quilt.

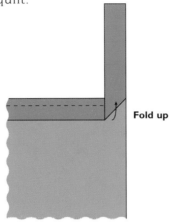

Fold the binding down even with the 2nd side of the quilt. Make sure the top fold is even with the 1st side of the quilt. Start sewing at the top and sew to within 1/4" of the next corner. Repeat.

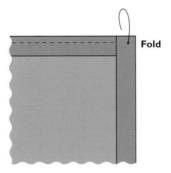

To finish the binding, turn the starting end of the binding strip under 1/4". Trim the end of the binding so it will tuck inside the fold of the unfinished binding. Sew the remaining unsewn portion of the binding to the quilt.

Fold the binding to the back of the quilt and blindstitch the binding to the quilt.

MACHINE APPLIQUÉ USING FUSIBLE ADHESIVE

Lay the fusible web sheet, paper-side up, on the pattern and trace with a pencil. Trace detail lines with a permanent marker for ease in transferring to the fabric.

Use paper-cutting scissors to roughly cut out the pieces. Leave at least a 1/4" border.

Following the manufacturer's instructions, fuse the web patterns to the wrong side of the appliqué fabric. It helps to use an appliqué-pressing sheet to avoid getting the adhesive on your iron or ironing board.

Cut out the pieces along the pencil line. Do not remove the paper yet.

Transfer the detail lines to the fabric by placing the piece on a light table or up to the window and marking the fabric with a pencil. Remove the paper and position the appliqué piece on your project.

Be sure the web (rough) side is down. Press in place, following the manufacturer's instructions.

PAPER PIECING

Once you get used to it, paper piecing is an easy way to ensure that your blocks are accurate. Sew on the side of the paper with the printed lines, with the fabric on the nonprinted side.

1. Trace or photocopy the number of paper-piecing patterns needed for your project.

2. Use a smaller-than-usual stitch length (#1.5–1.8, or 18 to 20 stitches per inch) and a slightly larger needle (size 90/14) to make paper removal easier and create tighter stitches that cannot be pulled apart when you tear the paper off.

3. Cut the pieces slightly larger than necessary—about $3/4$" larger. They do not need to be perfect shapes. (One of the joys of paper piecing!)

With paper piecing, you don't have to worry about the grain of the fabric. You are stitching on paper, and that stabilizes the block. The paper is not torn off until after the blocks are stitched together.

4. Follow the number sequence when piecing. Pin piece #1 in place on the blank side of the paper, but make sure you don't place the pin anywhere near a seamline. Hold the paper up to the light to ensure the piece covers the area it is supposed to, with the seam allowance also amply covered.

5. Fold the pattern back at the stitching line and trim the fabric to a $1/4$" seam allowance with a ruler and rotary cutter.

6. Cut piece #2 large enough to cover the area of #2 plus a generous seam allowance. It is a good idea to

cut each piece larger than you think necessary; it might be a bit wasteful, but it is easier than ripping out tiny stitches! Align the edge with the trimmed seam allowance of piece #1, right sides together, and pin. Paper side up, stitch 1 line.

7. Open piece #2 and press.

8. Continue stitching each piece in order, being sure to fold back the paper pattern and trim the seam allowance to $1/4$" before adding the next piece.

9. Trim all around the finished unit to the $1/4$" seam allowance. Leave the paper intact until after the blocks have been sewn together, then carefully remove it. Creasing the paper at the seamline helps when tearing it.

Paper Piecing Hints

When making several identical blocks, it helps to work in assembly-line fashion. Add pieces #1 and #2 to each of the blocks, then add #3, and so on.

Precutting the pieces all at once is a time saver. Precutting instructions for the pieces are given in the cutting chart for each project.

When piecing a dark and a light fabric together and when the seam allowance needs to be pressed toward the light fabric, the edge of the dark seam allowance will sometimes show through the light fabric. To prevent this, trim the dark seam allowance about $1/16$" narrower than the light seam allowance.

Resources

Elisa's Back Porch
Quarter Circle Templates
Fool's Puzzle Template
505-897-1894
www.backporchfabrics.com

Jukebox Quilts
P.O. Box 1518
Tustin, CA 92781-1518
714-731-2563
Notions, Threads & Inks
Kelly@Jukeboxquilts.com

Leath Enterprises Custom Templates
915-C West Foothill Blvd. #493
Claremont, CA 91711
800-515-4546
909-625-4546
Rlea@msn.com
www.notions4less.com

Quilters Dream Batting
589 Central Drive
Virginia Beach, VA 23454
757-463-3264
www.quiltersdreambatting.com

Rainbow Fabrics (Hand Dyes)
Diana Lacy
Oceanside, CA
www.RainbowFabrics.com

Superior Threads
P.O. Box 1672
St. George, UT 84771
800-499-1777
www.superiorthreads.com

Tools for Quilts with Curves
2549-B Eastbluff Dr. #123
Newport Beach, CA 92660
949-721-0865
email: justcurves@earthlink.net

*For more information,
ask for a free catalog:*
C&T Publishing, Inc.
P.O. Box 1456
Lafayette, CA 94549
(800) 284-1114
Email:ctinfo@ctpub.com
Website: www.ctpub.com

For quilting supplies:
Cotton Patch Mail Order
3405 Hall Lane, Dept. CTB
Lafayette, CA 94549
(800) 835-4418
(925) 283-7883
Email: quiltusa@yahoo.com
Website: www.quiltusa.com

Note: Fabrics used in the quilts shown may not be currently available because fabric manufacturers keep most fabrics in print for only a short time.

List of Publications from Earlene Fowler
Berkley Prime Crime
Penguin-Putnam Publishing

FOOL'S PUZZLE, ISBN: 0-425-14545-X

IRISH CHAIN, ISBN: 0-425-15137-9

KANSAS TROUBLES, ISBN: 0-425-15696-6

GOOSE IN THE POND, ISBN: 0-425-16239-7

DOVE IN THE WINDOW, ISBN: 0-425-16894-8

MARINER'S COMPASS, ISBN: 0-425-17408-5

SEVEN SISTERS, ISBN: 0-425-17296-1

ARKANSAS TRAVELER, ISBN: 0-425-17808-0

STEPS TO THE ALTAR, ISBN: 0-425-18349-1

SUNSHINE AND SHADOW, ISBN: 0-425-18855-8

BROKEN DISHES, ISBN: 0-425-19597-X

Mariner's Compass won the Agatha award for Best Novel of 1999.
Arkansas Traveler was number 8 on the *Los Angeles Times* Bestseller list.
Steps to the Altar was number 29 on the *New York Times* extended Bestseller list.
Sunshine and Shadow was number 31 on the *New York Times* Extended Bestseller list.

Index

About the Authors

Earlene Fowler, a native Californian, was raised in La Puente, California, by a Southern mother and a Western father. She wrote literary and commercial short fiction for ten years with no publishing success when she decided to change gaits and write a mystery novel. Her first novel, *Fool's Puzzle*, and two sequels were sold within a week of submission to Putnam-Berkley Publishing Group as one of three lead titles for their new hard-cover mystery line, Prime Crime. *Fool's Puzzle* was nominated for an Agatha award for Best First Novel of 1994. It was followed by *Irish Chain, Kansas Troubles, Goose in the Pond, Dove in the Window, Mariner's Compass, Seven Sisters, Arkansas Traveler, Steps to the Altar,* and *Sunshine and Shadow.*

Kansas Troubles, Goose in the Pond, Dove in the Window, Mariner's Compass, and *Arkansas Traveler* were each nominated for an Agatha award for Best Novel. *Mariner's Compass* won the Agatha for Best Novel of 1999.

Her quilt-titled mystery series starring Benni Harper, rancher and folk art museum curator, is set on the central coast of California in a town pointedly similar to San Luis Obispo. Fowler is an avid lover of quilts, folk art, horses, dogs, oral history, the Central Coast, country/western music, and cowboy boots (she owns 25 pair).

She is a member of Sisters in Crime and American Crime Writer's League organizations. She is a longtime instructor at the Cuesta College Writers' Conference in San Luis Obispo and has taught numerous writing seminars for libraries, Sisters in Crime, Mystery Writers of America conventions, and various other organizations. She has been a guest speaker at the Long Beach Literary Women and the Orange County Literary Guild events. She is a registered LIVE at the library speaker (affiliated with the American Library Association) and has spoken about writing, quilting, and creativity at dozens of libraries, quilt guilds, women's clubs, and charity events across the United States.

She has just completed book number eleven—*Broken Dishes*—which will be published in May 2004. She is currently working on book number twelve—*Delectable Mountains*. She lives in Orange County, California with her husband, Allen.

From an early age, **Margrit Hall** has had a desire to express herself artistically. She worked in a number of different mediums, but couldn't find the right means of expression. About thirty years ago she finally found her artistic voice—in quilting. Once she found that voice, she began to read and learn everything she could about her new passion. It wasn't long until others started asking for her assistance. With a college background in education and communications, sharing her enthusiasm and knowledge of quilting with others was a natural step.

Margrit began teaching quilting in 1982, first at Heritage Quilt store in Cheyenne, Wyoming, then at Laramie County Community College in Cheyenne. She specializes in quilting history and design technique.

"Although part of my focus is on teaching good, basic technique," she says, "my main goal is to introduce my students to the sheer joy of creating with fabric."

Having found her artistic voice she has continued to broaden and expand her talents. She used sketching and drawing as a means of transferring her thoughts and ideas to paper and then to fabric. She also began to express herself in watercolors as a means to visualize the colors in her designs. In 1995, fabric companies (Hoffman and RJR) took notice of her designs and asked her to design quilts to market their new fabric lines. She now designs original quilts and patterns under the name Cat Tail Designs. Her creations combine her love of watercolor painting with the feel and freedom of expression provided by fabric.

Margrit spent five years as curator of the Hoffman Challenge, a position she found both rewarding and inspiring. She is currently special projects director for Kaufman Fabrics. Her original patterns have been published in *McCall's Quilting Magazine, Quilter's Newsletter Magazine, Quilting Today,* and other quilt-related publications. She continues to be one of the featured quilt designers in the new Better Homes and Gardens quilt catalog. Her quilts have also been shown in invitational gallery exhibits.

She is currently a resident of Orange County, California where she lives with her husband, David, and where she continues to teach, lecture, and design.

appli-curves

Traditional Quilts with
EASY NO-SEW CURVES

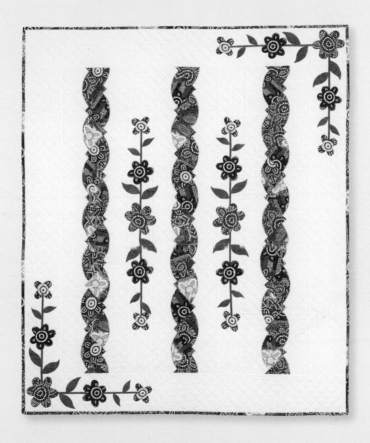

Elaine Waldschmitt

CINCINNATI, OHIO

www.MyCraftivity.com

Connect. Create. Explore.

about the author

Other fine Krause Publications are available from your local bookstore, craft supply store or online retailer, or visit our Web site at www.fwpublications.com.

12 11 10 09 08   5 4 3 2 1

DISTRIBUTED IN CANADA BY FRASER DIRECT
100 Armstrong Avenue
Georgetown, ON, Canada L7G 5S4
Tel: (905) 877-4411

DISTRIBUTED IN THE U.K. AND EUROPE BY DAVID & CHARLES
Brunel House, Newton Abbot, Devon, TQ12 4PU, England
Tel: (+44) 1626 323200, Fax: (+44) 1626 323319
Email: postmaster@davidandcharles.co.uk

DISTRIBUTED IN AUSTRALIA BY CAPRICORN LINK
P.O. Box 704, S. Windsor NSW, 2756 Australia
Tel: (02) 4577-3555

Library of Congress Cataloging-in-Publication Data
Waldschmitt, Elaine.
  Appli-curves : traditional quilts with easy no-sew curves / Elaine Waldschmitt.
    p. cm.
  Includes index.
  ISBN-13: 978-0-89689-601-7 (pbk. : alk. paper)
  ISBN-10: 0-89689-601-3 (pbk. : alk. paper)
  1. Patchwork—Patterns. 2. Machine quilting—Patterns. I. Title.
  TT835.W3363 2008
  746.46'041—dc22   2008030055

Edited by Stefanie Laufersweiler
Designed by Nicole Armstrong
Production coordinated by Matthew Wagner

As a little girl, Elaine Waldschmitt grew up watching her grandmother stitching hand-appliquéd quilts during the cold Minnesota winter nights. When she was 9, Elaine joined a 4-H group and learned to sew. For a high school graduation gift, she received her first sewing machine from her parents.

Throughout the next fifteen years, Elaine fell in love, married, was blessed with three active sons and kept advancing in her career as a registered dietitian. By 1995, she was a full-time neonatal nutritionist at the local children's hospital and a busy wife and mother.

Elaine began her pattern line, The Quilted Closet, in the fall of 1995, with four quilted jacket patterns. Each year, she designs and publishes new patterns, with her line now boasting over ninety patterns and seven books. In 2000, Elaine began designing quilting fabrics, and she is now licensed with Andover Fabrics. She teaches nationally and has frequently appeared as a guest of PBS quilting shows including *Sewing with Nancy* and *Kaye's Quilting Friends*.

Elaine lives in Johnston, Iowa. *Appli-Curves* is her first book with Krause Publications.

acknowledgments

As they say about raising a child: "It takes a village." Although the author of this book is only one person, it really took a village to make it happen! My heartfelt thanks to everyone in my "village," and my sincere apologies if there is anyone I may have overlooked.

The biggest acknowledgment of all goes to my husband, Jim, and my sons, Craig, Andrew and Ben, for allowing me to realize my dreams. I love you all more than you know.

Secondly, I'd like to thank all the fans and customers of The Quilted Closet patterns, who over the years have offered praise and encouragement that kept me going during the tough times.

I want to thank Rosella Hanson for introducing me to the "easy Drunkard's Path," and for her great work, inspiration and ideas. I miss seeing her and her beautiful work.

Many thanks to Krause Publications: Candy Wiza, for giving me the chance to present my proposal; Erica Swanson, my first editor; and Stefanie Laufersweiler, for finishing up the book with me. A special thanks to Laura Miller for her ideas and support.

Much gratitude goes to Bernina of America, especially Jeanne Delpit, for making sure I had a dream machine to work and create with.

All of the awesome fabrics in this book came from either Andover Fabrics or Starr Design Fabrics. Especially to David Winestein, Gail Kessler and Cliff Quibell at Andover Fabrics: a huge hug. You are an incredible group and I feel honored to work with you. Kathleen and Shelley Starr at Starr Design Fabrics produce gorgeous hand-dyed fabric I can't get enough of. Thanks for supplying fabrics not only for the projects, but also for the step-by-step illustrations. You are true friends and special people.

My great appreciation goes to Bob and Heather Purcell, owners of Superior Threads, who have taught me most of what I know about threads. Your threads have made a difference in my quilting and in all my sewing and embellishing projects.

The beautiful quilting on most of the quilts in this book was done by Val Sjoblom from On A Wing & A Prayer. Thanks for always fitting me in and meeting my deadlines. I couldn't have done it without you, and your quilting is gorgeous!

And last but not least, I want to acknowledge my buddy Leah, my Golden Retriever who never leaves my side, and my new girlfriend Lucy, my goldendoodle puppy, who has become a second constant companion. Woof! (That was "thanks" in dog talk.)

dedication

To my late grandmother, Claire, for introducing me to the world of quilting. I love and miss you, Grandma.

To my sister, Laurel, for planting the seed and helping it grow. I love you like no other.

Metric Conversion Chart

To convert	to	multiply by
Inches	Centimeters	2.54
Centimeters	Inches	0.4
Feet	Centimeters	30.5
Centimeters	Feet	0.03
Yards	Meters	0.9
Meters	Yards	1.1

table of contents

introduction

I still remember that "aha" moment when a friend told me how to make a "cheater" Drunkard's Path. I had long used fusible web for appliquéing quick projects, but it had never occurred to me that the fusible web could be used where I had formerly only considered piecing. I remember thinking, "Oh, I can do that!"

In my first quilting class nearly thirty years ago, there was not a sewing machine in the shop. There were six of us, and we were taught how to thread and knot our needles for hand-piecing. I knew I had fallen in love with quilting that very moment. Piecing the straight seams was easy enough, but when the teacher showed us the Drunkard's Path block at a later class, I wondered if my seams would match when I attempted to piece the curves. After all, the two tiny pieces to be joined

curved in opposite directions! I remember being one of the few in the class who ended up with a perfect curve. I had relied on my days of garment sewing and tailoring, and was good with the needle. I even grew to love the challenge of the curved seams, as the straight pieced seams got a little boring at times.

But as my life progressed into busier times, I found myself doing more and more machine piecing, machine quilting and less handwork. I now was raising a family, and life had little spare time. I also found myself avoiding blocks with curves; I knew they were a little challenging and I'd prefer to piece them by hand. I watched many demos on curved piecing templates and learned about curved piecing presser feet, but none of them held great appeal. Somehow I just couldn't get excited about them. For the most part, I'd become a machine piecer and I avoided curves. That's why that "aha" moment was so prominent. The first time I used the technique, I was in love with it! Curves were now stress-free, and the results were perfect every time.

The Appli-Curves method changed my attitude entirely. I have been making curved pieced blocks, from simple to complex, with no hesitation since that discovery, loving the process as much as the results. I started to look at blocks differently, seeing how this method could fit into so many traditional blocks. Best of all, I learned that anyone can be successful with this method the first time they try.

I've chosen just three simple blocks to include in this book. I hope after you examine the method, read through this book and try it for yourself, you'll begin to see all the possibilities for curved pieced blocks and expand your creativity as much as I have mine.

LET'S BEGIN!

Probably most (or all) of the supplies you'll need to be successful with Appli-Curves are already stocked in your sewing room. Anything you don't have and need to purchase, you will probably use over and over for other projects. This is a machine-stitched technique, so be sure your sewing machine is in good working order and you have a supply of new machine needles and a variety of threads. (More on needles and threads later in this chapter.) Of course, you'll need an ironing station and basic quilting/sewing supplies, such as scissors, pins, rotary cutter, rulers and a mat. You will need a standard pencil as well as a fabric marking pencil or chalk.

The defining tool for the Appli-Curves method is the fusible web, which is discussed in detail on page 17. Because you will be using fusible web, an appliqué-pressing sheet is a must. This handy tool protects your iron and ironing surface from getting gummed up. It is semi-transparent, allowing you to place templates under it to assist in fabric placement.

threads

As a beginning quilter, I didn't place threads high on my list of concerns. It was all about the fabric, the technique and finishing! Over the years, I've learned just how much a correct thread can impact my final results. Now I know that thread affects the look of my project, what needle I choose (or don't choose), and how well my tension is performing. A high-quality thread will not break easily or shred, and it will perform well.

There are many wonderful threads available to quilters today. For the beginner, choosing threads can seem overwhelming. Color is certainly one of the greatest determinants, but there is much more to be considered. A poor thread choice can affect the look of your finished quilt, and a good choice is crucial to the success of this technique. Understanding the thread fiber content, weight and quality can simplify your thread decisions.

COLOR

With this method, thread color is a very important factor. You can change the feel of your project merely with your color selection. Since the Appli-Curves method is meant to emulate traditional hand-piecing, often you will want to match the thread to your fabric. This lets the thread "melt" into the raw edge and not detract from the fabrics and design of the quilt block. On the other hand, you may want to use your threads as another design element. In this case, consider some of the beautiful variegated threads. Combined with a decorative stitch, this can be just the right accent to personalize your block and make it uniquely yours.

When thinking about thread color, look at your fused block. Ask yourself, "Does this block need further embellishment with thread to enhance it, or would seeing thread detract from the look of the block?" You'll know immediately. In most cases I want my threads to hide, to function rather than embellish on the block. After all, I'm aiming for that traditional look in an

Use 0.004 nylon monofilament thread and a small needle for an invisible look. A monofilament polyester can perform similarly to 0.004 nylon.

easier format. However, sometimes a non-matching thread color will add the perfect touch.

SIZE AND WEIGHT

Without getting too technical, weight is one aspect used to determine the size of a thread. A lighter thread will blend into the fabric (and be more invisible). A heavier thread is less able to imbed into the fabric and tends to be more noticeable on the top of the work. The weight of a thread is actually based on a length measurement: how much thread can fit around a certain spool. The smaller the number, the heavier the thread. This makes sense, because you'll be able to wind less of a heavier thread on a spool than a lighter one.

For Appli-Curves, the thread weight I choose depends on my desired result. For stitching the curves I want to look invisible, I prefer a lighter 40-weight thread. I want the thread to blend in, especially with the tiny zigzag, blanket or buttonhole stitch. When using decorative stitches for edge finishing, I usually want my thread to show, so I'll choose a heavier thread, such as a 30-weight.

If you are hesitant to experiment with decorative threads, don't worry—almost every thread will work. Success is related to how the thread interacts with

Use variegated thread to add further embellishment to a block.

the machine, the needle and the fabric. If you have trouble with a thread, one or a combination of these factors are the cause. This can be hard to accept in the midst of broken needles, tethered thread and ripping out stitches; however, when you take the time to use the thread properly, you will find that it performs well. Many decorative threads cannot be sewn at the high speed of today's newer sewing machines, so slow

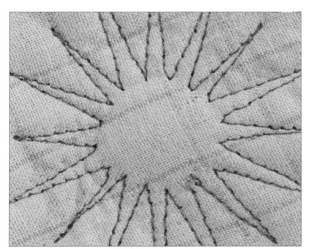

Thread makes a difference!

Trilobal polyester and rayon threads have a glossy sheen that may or may not be desirable on your project.

down. Use a larger needle and be sure it's an embroidery needle, which will help protect the thread as it intersects with the fabric. Adjust the tension on your machine as needed, and stitch out practice samples until you obtain the desired results. Remember, using decorative thread can significantly enhance the block—sometimes it's worth a little extra time to get this unique and special effect.

BOBBIN THREADS

I used to use up all my old threads in my bobbin because I didn't think the bobbin thread mattered;

and in many cases, it probably doesn't. But when stitching the raw edges of the curves, the bobbin thread will play a role in whether your finished block can look like a traditionally pieced block.

For finishing raw curved edges, a fine, light bobbin thread is most effective. Most of the time you will want the stitching to melt into the block, not detract from the block. If you use a too-heavy bobbin thread, this will add bulk and "raise" the curved edge. This accentuates and draws attention to the stitching on the curved edge.

The bobbin thread is independent of the top thread—they do not need to match in fiber content or in size. For Appli-Curves, I prefer to use a lightweight

2-ply, 60-weight or "Bobbin Weight" threads work best in the bobbin for the Appli-Curves method.

Some machines allow you to make adjustments on the bobbin case to fine-tune the tension.

bobbin thread such as two-ply or 60-weight, as this still provides sufficient strength without adding bulk. I usually purchase bobbin threads in standard colors like off-white and gray in large cones to save on cost. These colors work well in almost all projects.

TENSION AND STITCH QUALITY

Many variables exist every time you sit down at your sewing machine. The top thread, bobbin thread, fabric and needle you have chosen for the project all influence the tension. Lightweight threads put little tension on the tension discs, whereas a heavy thread actually pushes harder against the tension discs when it is in your machine. Follow manufacturer's instructions to make adjustments to obtain the best stitch quality. Don't be afraid to experiment! You can't hurt your machine by adjusting the tension, and your machine can't always self-adjust to the variables you present to it.

needles

Many experts recommend inserting a new needle each time you start a project. I certainly agree. The needle is a key player in your sewing success, and tiny bends and burrs often aren't noticeable to your eye. The size and type of needle you choose for Appli-Curves will vary, depending on the desired result. When the goal is invisibility, use a smaller needle, such as a size 60/8 or 75/11. The combination of the small needle and the lighter thread brings amazing results. The size 60/8 or 75/11 needle will leave a smaller hole when it pierces between the fibers of the fabric, which will give your piece a more delicate or invisible look. This is especially important on the tiny zigzag edge finish. Needles that are too large can cause the fibers of your fabric to separate and fray, which is significant due to the small width of the zigzag stitch.

However, if you are using a decorative thread, you may be unable to use the smaller needle. For decorative threads, I recommend an embroidery needle, which will protect the thread and give better performance. Understanding sewing machine needles and having an assortment available to you at all times will bring better results with all your sewing.

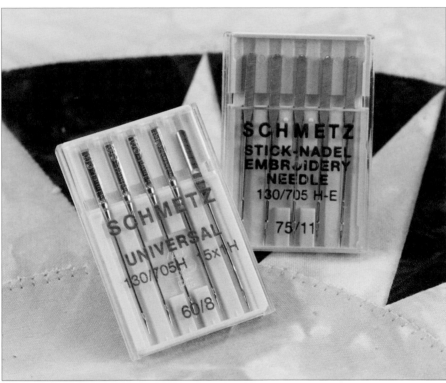

Don't underestimate the role of a good-quality needle. A 60/8 or 75/11 needle will produce more invisible-looking results than a larger needle.

fusible web

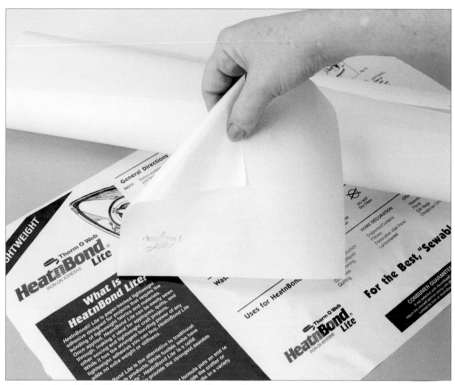

My favorite brand of fusible web. Be sure to follow the manufacturer's instructions, no matter what brand you use.

To make the projects in this book, you will need paper-backed fusible (iron-on) web. This is a paper-backed adhesive that will bond fabrics with the heat of your iron. It must be paper-backed so that you can draw on the web with a pencil. Paper-backed fusible webs come in many varieties: light, medium or heavy weight, and no-sew or sewable. Of all the supplies discussed in this chapter, your selection of this product will be the most important to your success. The web will become a part of your quilt, so being sure the product performs properly, not only at the time of construction, but also years from now after washing, use and love, is extremely important. Choose the right product, and it will be worth the time and energy in the long run. I have used Therm O Web HeatnBond Lite for decades, and I highly recommend it. I have projects with HeatnBond Lite

that I have washed weekly, and the bond has held up well through all the washings, season after season. This brand has also been predictable in its performance, with the adhesive always reacting to the heat consistently and the paper never separating before I want it to.

Unless it is unavoidable, always choose a lightweight fusible web. Even the lightweight variety will add a significant amount of stiffness to your project. Choose a product that says it can be sewn through. The no-sew varieties are not intended to be sewn, and they may gum up your needle or cause problems with the inner workings of your sewing machine.

Fusible web is sold by the yard in your local quilt shop. It is available in various widths and packaging, but most commonly it is about 17" (43cm) wide.

general instructions

- Please read all instructions before beginning.
- Cut strips across the width of the fabric. The usable width is about 42" (107cm).
- Cut the fabric in the order listed.
- All measurements, unless noted, are based on ¼" (6mm) seams, and all piecing is completed with right sides facing. After piecing, press seam allowances to one side, the darker side when possible.
- Due to potential problems with shrinkage and color bleeding, consider prewashing all fabric before beginning the projects.
- Whenever you are pressing where fusible web may be exposed, be sure to use your appliqué-pressing sheet so you don't gum up your iron and/or your ironing board.

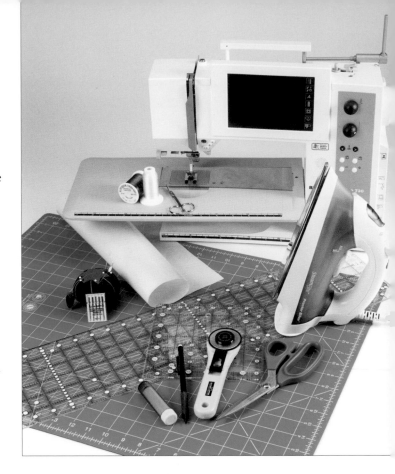

MITERING BORDERS

A beautifully mitered border adds to a quilt's charm. The Floral Parade Quilt on page 80 has a wide floral border, and it must be mitered in order to properly frame the quilt. One important part of mitering borders is making sure the border ends are left long enough to complete the miter. Mitered borders require more fabric than straight borders, and they can be a little more challenging. Follow these instructions for success.

1 Be sure the border ends are long enough for the miter. (For specific border lengths on the Floral Parade Quilt, see instructions on page 80.)

Mark exactly ¼" (6mm) from each corner.

2 Using a fabric-marking pencil, mark a dot in each corner of the quilt top exactly ¼" (6mm) from the edge.

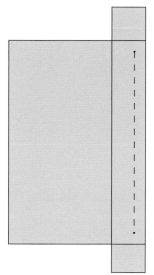

Backstitch at the dots.

3 Center the border strips to the center of the side. Using ¼" (6mm) seams, attach the borders, stopping at the dot, and backstitch to secure. Do not stitch past the dot on any corner.

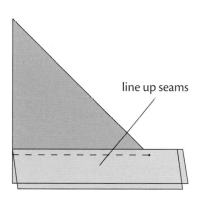

line up seams

4 Fold the quilt top on the diagonal with right sides together. Match the raw edges of the borders and seams, allowing the border ends to extend straight out from the quilt. Pin the border ends securely.

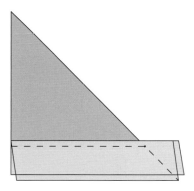

5 Using a ruler with a 45-degree marking, line up the 45-degree edge so it extends directly from the dot. The horizontal lines on the ruler should match the seam lines. Use a pencil to mark the 45-degree angle onto the border ends, so the line extends directly from the dot.

6 Stitch on the drawn line without stitching into the dot. (I like to use a very long basting stitch for my first pass, then open up the quilt; if I like the results, I re-stitch over the basting stitch with a regular stitch length.) Backstitch at the beginning and end of the stitching.

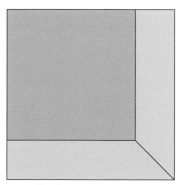

Mitered border.

7 If the miter looks good and there are no puckers, trim the seam to ¼" (6mm) and press the seam open. Repeat for all of the border corners.

BASIC BLOCK-MAKING:
THE APPLI-CURVES METHOD

This chapter will walk you through the basic construction of each of the three blocks used in this book, step by step. Acquaint yourself with these methods prior to beginning any of the projects. The basic technique is the same for all of the projects. However, there are slight variations for each block: the Drunkard's Path, the Hearts and Gizzards or the New York Beauty block. In all three blocks, the curves are drawn onto the paper side of fusible web, and then fused onto a base fabric. Because fusible web work leaves a raw edge, you will need to finish that raw edge with stitching. For Drunkard's Path and the Hearts and Gizzards blocks, you will need to sub-cut to actually obtain the final block. For the New York Beauty, the center arcs are paper-pieced. Also, in all three blocks it is important to reduce the bulk created by extra fabric and paper-backed fusible web.

2

drunkard's path block

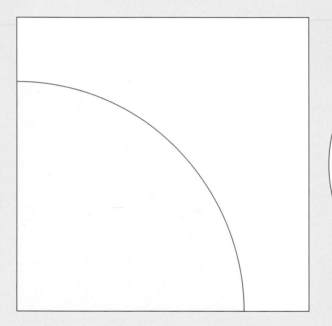

DRUNKARD'S PATH
CIRCLE SHAPE

The Drunkard's Path block is a simple two-color patch. With the Appli-Curves method, four identical Drunkard's Path blocks are generated at one time. Choose two contrasting fabrics and locate Template 2 on the CD to get started.

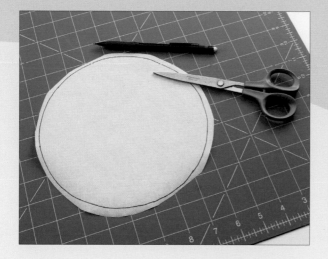

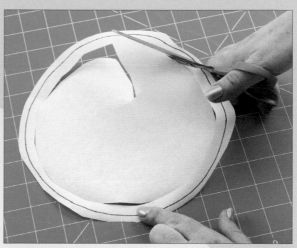

1 Print Template 2 from the CD and trace it onto the paper side of the fusible web. Cut out the paper circle approximately ¼" (6mm) outside of the tracing lines.

2 Trim away the inside of each paper circle, leaving about ¼" (6mm) on the inside of the tracing line.

tip

Trimming the paper from inside the circle is not necessary, but it will remove most of the fusible web from the project and leave your quilt softer. The ¼" (6mm) of fusible web on the edge serves as a stabilizer for your stitching.

3 Being careful not to distort the circle shape, fuse the paper "ring" onto the wrong side of the 9" (23cm) square fabric. Cut out the shape on the pencil line.

4 Fold both the circle and the 9½" (24cm) background square in fourths to find their centers. Lightly finger press.

5 Pierce the center of the circle shape with a straight pin, and then pierce into the center of background square, keeping the fabric perpendicular to the pin to match exact centers.

6 Fuse the circle shape onto the background square.

7 Finish the raw edges of the circle with stitching. Begin the stitching at either the 3, 6, 9 or 12 o'clock position. This will ensure the stitching is continuous across each curve (with no knots) once the block is cut.

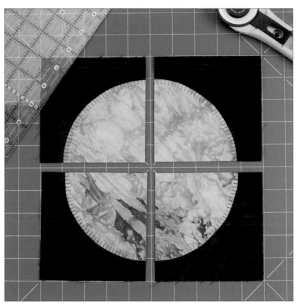

8 Using a rotary cutter and transparent ruler, cut the block vertically and horizontally in the exact center to produce four identical Drunkard's Path blocks.

9 Using scissors, carefully trim the background fabric behind the circle to reduce bulk.

hearts and gizzards block

MATERIALS

To make two blocks:

- 8¾" (22cm) square light fabric for background
- 8¾" (22cm) square dark fabric for background
- 7" × 14" (18cm x 36cm) rectangle (approximately) each of light and dark fabrics for Template 13
- ½ yd. (46cm) paper-backed fusible web
- Thread to match or contrast fabrics

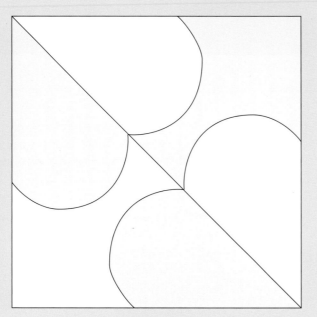

HEART SHAPE

Hearts and Gizzards is also a two-color block, but it is set in a positive-negative arrangement. Pieced with traditional methods, this block requires four curved seams plus a straight seam. With the Appli-Curves method, two identical blocks are generated at once with no curved piecing.

Begin with a square each of light and dark fabric, fusible web and thread to match the fabrics. Use Template 13 from the CD.

26

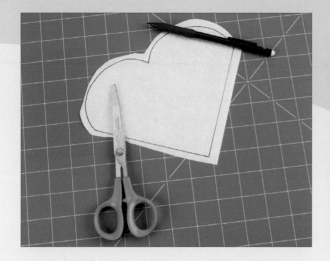

1 Print Template 13 from the CD. Trace four templates (heart shapes) onto the paper side of the fusible web, leaving at least ½" (1cm) between the shapes. Cut out the paper shapes approximately ¼" (6mm) outside of the tracing lines.

2 Trim away the inside of each paper heart, leaving about ¼" (6mm) on the inside of the tracing line.

tip

Trimming the paper from inside the heart shape is not necessary, but it will remove most of the fusible web from the project and leave your quilt softer. The ¼" (6mm) of fusible web on the edge serves as a stabilizer for your stitching.

3 Being careful not to distort the heart shape, fuse a paper "heart ring" onto the wrong side of the dark fabric (for template), and cut the shape on the pencil lines. Repeat to prepare two dark fabric hearts, then make two light fabric hearts.

4 Arrange, and then fuse two light hearts onto the dark 8¾" (22cm) fabric square, matching the hearts at the opposite diagonal corners. Arrange, and then fuse two dark hearts onto the light 8¾" (22cm) fabric square, matching the hearts on opposite diagonal corners.

5 Stitch the curved raw edges of the hearts.

6 On the back of each block, trim the fabric under the heart. This will reduce the bulk when you are seaming the blocks.

 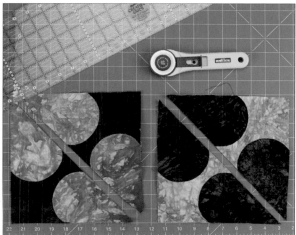

7 Using a rotary cutter and transparent ruler, cut the blocks on the diagonal through the centers of the hearts.

8 Using a ¼" (6mm) seam, join the triangles of opposite colors to create two Hearts and Gizzards blocks. If desired, trim the "ears" from the ends of the diagonal seam. This will also reduce bulk when joining the blocks.

new york beauty block

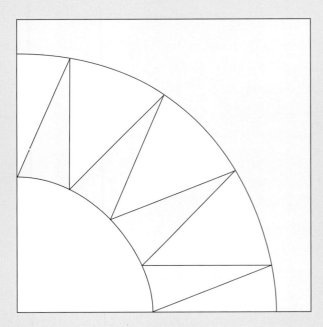

Traditionally, this block required hand-piecing not just for the curves, but also to obtain sharp points on the spikes. Paper-piecing the spikes is a quick, yet accurate alternative. The Appli-Curves technique on the curved edges assures a no-fail result in a fraction of the time for traditional methods.

This block is more difficult than the others. My methods were developed, then fine-tuned as I got better and better at making the blocks. Several quilt testers have used this method, and it's unanimous that this method produces the best foolproof results, with the greatest ease. I have presented two methods for the New York Beauty block: one for first-timers with the block (Method 1), the other when you are comfortable with the technique (Method 2). There are advantages and disadvantages to both, as discussed. Both methods begin with a completed paper-pieced arc (instructions follow), and then the curved edges are fused onto the arc.

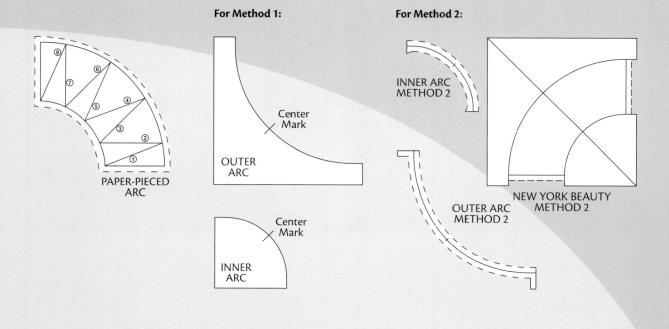

For Method 1:

PAPER-PIECED ARC

OUTER ARC — Center Mark

INNER ARC — Center Mark

For Method 2:

INNER ARC METHOD 2

OUTER ARC METHOD 2

NEW YORK BEAUTY METHOD 2

Paper-Piece the Arcs

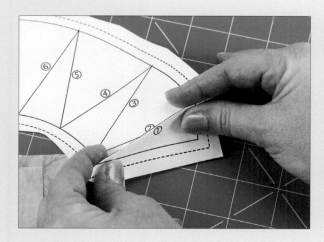

1 Print Template 18 from the CD and trim about ¼" (6mm) outside of the dotted lines. Locate Line 1 and fold the paper on this line. This fold serves as a marking so you know where to place your fabric. You'll arrange your fabric on the *unprinted* side and sew on the *printed* side.

2 Turn the paper printed-side down. Lay a 2" × 5" (5cm × 13cm) background fabric rectangle (pink) and a spike fabric rectangle (red) right sides together, background fabric on the bottom, matching the 5" (13cm) edges on the right.

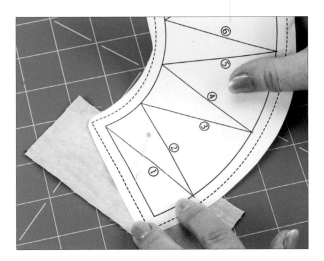

3 Lay the rectangles ¼"–½" (6mm–1cm) over the fold in the paper. Pin across the fold. Turn so the paper side is up.

4 Using a small stitch length, stitch on Line 1 through the paper and both fabrics. Start and stop stitching just off the paper. If you use a very short stitch, it will be much easier to remove the paper later on.

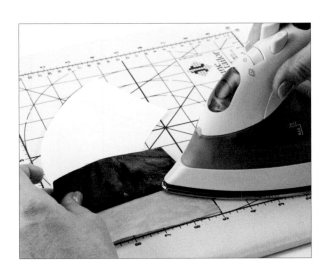

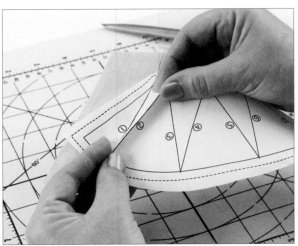

5 Press the rectangles open. Check to make sure the spike fabric covers the entire area between lines 1 and 2. Trim the seam allowance to ¼" (6mm), and press the rectangles open again.

6 Turn so the printed side is facing up. Fold the paper on Line 2.

Completed arc, front side

7 Lay a 3" × 5" (8cm × 13cm) background rectangle over the spike fabric, right sides facing, so the edge extends ¼"–½" (6mm–1cm) beyond the folded crease on the template paper. Pin across the fold. Turn so the printed side is facing up. Stitch on Line 2.

8 Turn over, open and press. Trim the seam allowance to ¼" (6mm). Turn the paper over and crease Line 3. Continue adding rectangles, alternating the background and spike fabrics to finish piecing the arc.

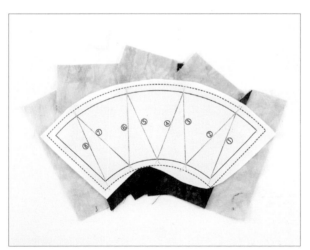

Completed arc, back side

9 Trim away the excess fabric to be even with the dotted lines. Do not remove the paper until instructed to do so for Method 1 or 2.

Add Inner and Outer Arcs

Choose either Method 1 or 2. *Note:* Use your appliqué pressing sheet for the following steps (Method 1 or 2) to prevent fusible web from gumming up your iron or your ironing surface.

Method 1

This method is good for beginners, or if you are trying the Appli-Curves method for the first time. You will have effortless success with this method, even though it does require more fabric and paper-backed fusible web. This method results in bulkier seams and leaves your quilt heavier and stiffer since the blocks contain more fabric and fusible web.

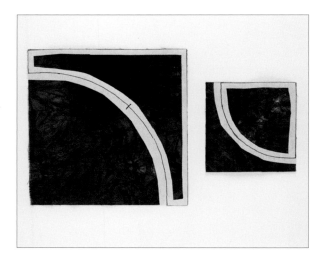

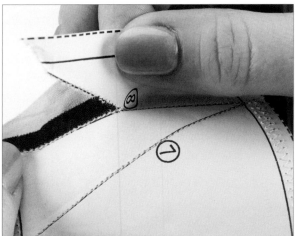

1 Print templates 16 and 17 from the CD. Trace one of each shape onto the paper side of the fusible web, leaving at least ¼" (6mm) extra between the shapes. Cut out each shape about ¼" (6mm) outside of the tracing lines. Trim the inside of each shape, leaving approximately ¼" (6mm) of fusible web inside the lines. Fuse the outer arc "ring" onto the back of the 7" (18cm) square. Fuse the inner arc "ring" onto the back of the 4" (10cm) square, lining up the right-angle edges of the shapes with the fabrics' grain lines. Cut out the shapes on the pencil lines. Remove the paper backing.

2 Carefully remove the paper from your paper-pieced section. When pulling paper off the paper-pieced sections, hold your thumb over the end stitches to prevent them from unraveling.

tip

Trimming the paper from inside the arc shapes is not necessary, but it will remove most of the fusible web from the project and leave your quilt softer. The ¼" (6mm) of fusible web on the edge serves as a stabilizer for your stitching.

34

3 Bring the 7" (18cm) muslin square to the ironing surface. Position the paper-pieced arc onto the muslin, matching the arc and block diagonals to obtain accurate placement. A ¼" (6mm) piece of the muslin will be visible along the sides of the paper-pieced arc. Pin the arc to the muslin base.

4 Position the inner arc over the lower corner of the muslin, matching the straight edges of the muslin and the arc, as shown. The curved edge of the arc should lie at the points created by the bottoms of the spikes. Adjust the paper-pieced arc, if needed, so the points match.

5 Position the outer arc over the upper corner of the muslin, matching the edges, as shown. The curved edge of the outer arc should lie at the top points created by the spikes. Adjust the paper-pieced arc, if needed, so all the points match.

6 Fuse the inner and outer arcs onto the paper-pieced section and the muslin square. Use the pressing sheet under and over the block to avoid transferring fusible web to your iron or ironing surface. Carefully transfer the block to your sewing machine. Skip to page 38 for next steps.

Method 2

The second method is slightly more challenging. When you choose the second method, you will use less fabric and paper-backed fusible web, and your quilt will be lighter and softer. Be careful, though—Method 2 requires more precise positioning, cutting and sewing.

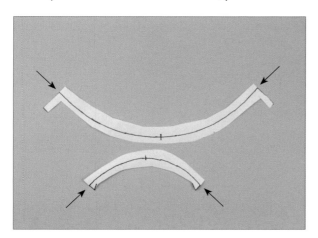

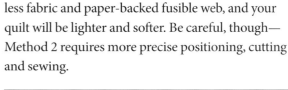

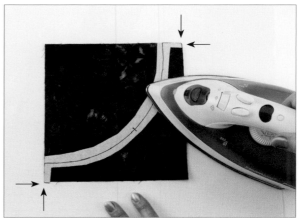

1 Print templates 16-2 and 17-2 from the CD. Trace one of each curve onto the paper side of the fusible web, leaving at least ½" (1cm) between shapes. Cut out the curves, leaving ¼" (6mm) outside the pencil lines. Trim exactly on the line on the ends only, as shown (see arrows).

2 Place the 7" (18cm) outer arc square wrong-side up on the pressing sheet. Fuse the outer arc onto the back of the 7" (18cm) square, lining up the curve's right-angle edges with the fabric's grain lines. The fusible web that you cut in step 1 should line up with the raw edges of the 7" (18cm) square, as shown (see arrows).

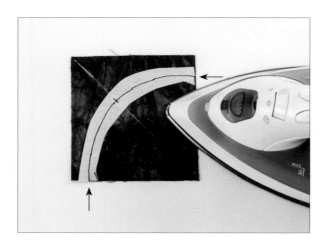

3 Position the inner arc in the same manner on the wrong side of the 4" (10cm) square, making sure to line up the edges, as shown (see arrows).

4 Cut each arc on the curved line, separating the two pieces. Save the leftover fabric for another project.

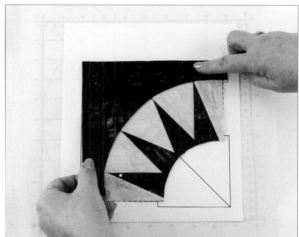

5 Print Template 19 from the CD onto letter-sized paper, then place the template under an appliqué-pressing sheet on the ironing surface. Using the template to assist, position the paper-pieced arc over the appropriate section. Use straight pins to hold, as shown. Pin directly onto the ironing surface to hold the patches as you arrange them.

6 Position the outer arc over the paper-pieced section, lining up the outer edges with the block template, and centering it over the paper-pieced section. Adjust so the tips of the spikes meet the edge of the outer arc.

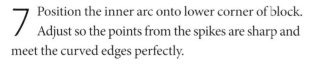

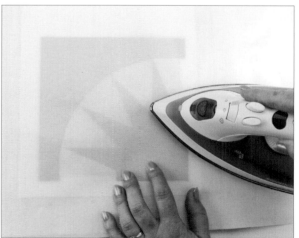

7 Position the inner arc onto lower corner of block. Adjust so the points from the spikes are sharp and meet the curved edges perfectly.

8 Cover the block with the second appliqué-pressing sheet. Fuse the block, being careful the parts do not shift as you press. Allow block to cool, then remove the block from the appliqué-pressing sheet.

Stitch and Square the Block

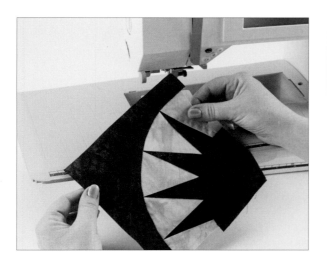

Nearly invisible stitching creates the illusion of a pieced curve.

1 Using matching or invisible nylon thread, stitch the edges of the inner and outer arc curves. Use the blanket or buttonhole stitch, or the tiny zigzag (see page 40). On this block, keeping this stitching as invisible as possible is the goal.

tip

When stitching around the curves, consider reducing motor speed to improve control. Use an open-toe foot, which allows you to see the needle while you are stitching. Be sure not to stretch the fabric as you stitch, since you are working with bias edges.

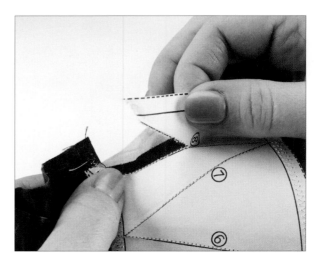

2 If you used Method 2, carefully remove the paper from the paper-pieced arc.

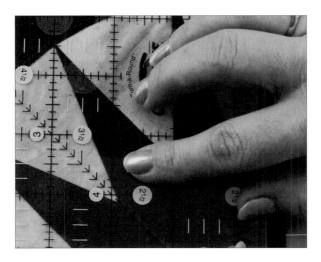

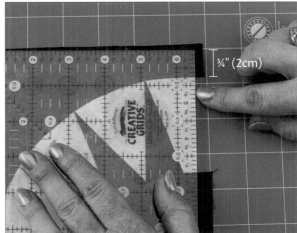

3 Your block is now approximately 7" (18cm), and it needs to be "squared up" to 6½" (17cm). This guarantees that the blocks are all perfectly sized, and that they will piece nicely into your project. Position the 6½" (17cm) diagonal ruler over the block and use the ruler markings to help you align the block. prior to trimming: 1) Line up the diagonal line on the ruler with the exact center of the middle two spikes; 2) Aim for ¾" (2cm) on each side from the top of the ruler to the invisible stitching on the curved edge, as shown.

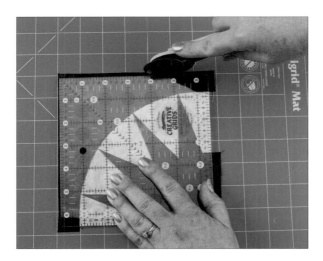

4 When your block is properly aligned, hold the ruler firmly and trim two adjacent sides without lifting the ruler. Lift the ruler, rotate the block, line up the trimmed edges with the edges of the ruler, and trim the remaining two sides so block is now perfectly centered and measures 6½" (17cm).

finishing raw edges

Perfectly finished edges on this block give the illusion of perfect piecing. Tiny zigzag stitches with carefully matched thread achieved this effect.

Even though many fusible webs available today have a no-sew option, a quilt is not secure unless you stitch around those curved edges. After all, there is nothing worse than seeing fraying, holes and separations in a quilt after you have finally finished it. Remember, over the course of its life, a quilt may be subjected to a lot of pulling, stretching and stress. Think about the stress on the fibers, stitching and threads when you sit on a bed covered with a quilt. The previously flat quilt now has to stretch under the weight of your body. Depending on the mattress, this can mean a great deal of stretch, easily lifting non-stitched areas.

To stitch, or not to stitch, is a personal preference, however. If you are making a wall hanging, you may choose to use a no-sew fusible web and not finish the edges. But for most applications, stitching the raw edges is a must. Stitching can also add personality, definition and beauty to your quilt.

Assuming you are going to stitch the edges, you will find yourself with many questions to ponder. What stitch should I use? What color thread will look

best? What type of thread is best? Should I use all one thread, or many different ones to match the fabric on the block?

First, let's talk about the stitch. You can use a tiny, invisible zigzag, the buttonhole or blanket stitch, or a decorative stitch from your sewing machine. Each of these stitches gives different results, requires different supplies and can be used to achieve a unique look.

TINY ZIGZAG STITCH

Use this method for nearly invisible stitching, or if the seam needs definition. This edge treatment is intended for function only. The purpose is to stitch the curve onto the patchwork with great ease for the stitcher, in the quickest time, providing the best long-term results. It is not intended to be decorative in any way. (In fact, it is meant to be invisible to most admirers.) The use of lightweight threads allows the threads to sink into the fabric, as opposed to lying on top, which heavier threads are forced to do. Using the open-toe foot allows you to see where to stitch easily—important since you are stitching all curves. The zigzag should not straddle the raw edge, but lie

The tiny zigzag stitch on the New York Beauty block. Using a perfectly matched thread with the tiny zigzag creates a nearly invisible stitch that blends into the fabric.

completely on the fused edge, ending right at the cut edge.

The success of this method will depend on how well you match the thread color to the fabric, the weights of the threads and the size of the needle.

Although you may think it's better to straddle the edge, I have found this leaves no room for error. The zigzag stitch is very small, and getting off just a little may leave areas unstitched, or stitched in such a way that stitches pull out when the quilt is stressed and pulled in use. By aiming for the entire zigzag stitch to lie on the fused fabric, you will still catch plenty of fabric, even if you stitch unevenly once in awhile.

Refer to the chart on page 42 for details on the tiny zigzag method.

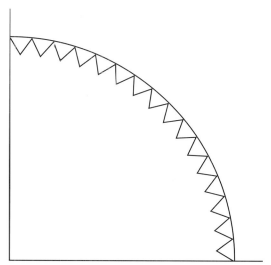

Keep the zigzag on the raw edge of the curve fabric. DON'T straddle the curve fabric.

DECORATIVE STITCH

This is a great way to finish your edges, especially on the Drunkard's Path or Hearts and Gizzards blocks. Most everyone has wonderful stitches on their sewing machines that would be perfect to use. These stitches will personalize your project and can add depth and texture to your patchwork. Try being more creative by using a variegated thread, as I did for the *Cabana Throw*, shown on page 64.

The tiny zigzag method was used on the Drunkard's Path block from the *Scarlet Sunset Throw* (page 52). The use of the solid thread defines the edge of the fabric and helps to contain its busy pattern.

On this Drunkard's Path block from the *Cabana Throw* (page 64), decorative thread and a decorative stitch were used as an embellishment.

BUTTONHOLE OR BLANKET STITCH

This is by far my favorite method of the three presented. Besides the pleasing look of the buttonhole stitch, I also feel that this stitch performs better on the bias curves of the patchwork. If the tension settings are not just perfect, or the threads and fabrics not perfectly matched, the zigzag method has occasionally resulted in some stretching. I never seem to see this when I use the buttonhole stitch.

Threads can be matched to the fabric, or one single color of thread can be used for the entire block.

When a single color is used (usually black), the stitch serves to define the edges of the curves much like the hand button-hold stitch that our ancestors used. I love the look of black buttonhole stitching on traditional appliqué, and this can be pleasing on your quilts as well. (I prefer it on the Drunkard's Path and Hearts and Gizzards projects, but feel it is distracting on the New York Beauty blocks.)

The buttonhole stitch takes a "bite" into the fused edge, with the base of the stitch hiding in the ditch of the fused edge and the background fabric. The length of the "bite" is personal preference. I like to assimilate the hand-stitched buttonhole, and so I use a large stitch width and length for my buttonhole stitching. Experiment on a scrap piece of block fabric and decide what settings work best for you.

The buttonhole stitch with a matching thread also gives a nearly invisible effect. This stitch seems to eliminate the chance of stretching when stitching the bias curves.

Instead of matching the threads to the fabric, a solid black thread was used on the *Barn Raising Framed Art* (page 58) to add definition.

Edge Finishing Suggestions

On this chart are my suggestions for stitching both the tiny zigzag stitch and the buttonhole or blanket stitch. Use it as a springboard for getting started until you develop your own favorite settings.

Stitch	Zigzag	Buttonhole or blanket
Stitch width	1–1.5	5.5
Stitch length	1.5–2	3.5
Upper thread	Two-ply cotton, rayon or polyester	Varies
Bobbin thread	Two-ply 100% polyester	Varies
Presser foot	Open-toe foot	Open-toe foot
Needle	60/8 or 75/11	60/8 or 75/11

reducing bulk

Because our curves are appliquéd, or layered onto the block, increased bulk becomes an issue. This problem is especially apparent on the Hearts and Gizzards block, where multiple seams are joined at the corners of the blocks. To reduce the bulk, the backing must be cut away behind the curves, just as in traditional appliqué.

Reduce the bulk in the blocks after the edges of the curves have been finished. Use appliqué scissors, if you have them, and proceed carefully. Be careful not to cut into the patchwork.

Drunkard's Path block.

Hearts and Gizzards block.

New York Beauty block.

DRUNKARD'S PATH: AN OLD FAVORITE

Prominent in historical quilt collections, the two-color Drunkard's Path block is very familiar to most quilters. Layout combinations are endless, and many layouts have earned their own names. According to folklore, the original name was inspired by the wobbly zigzag path created by some layouts, which obviously reminded our ancestors of someone who'd had too much to drink!

The block can be combined with other elements to create new blocks, such as the Spiced Pinks block featured in the *Harvest Bloom Table Runner* on page 72, or the simple spinning block used in the *Twirly Bird Table Runner* on page 46.

3

twirly bird table runner

MATERIALS

- ⅓ yd. (30cm) white solid fabric
- ¼ yd. (23cm) each of two different green prints for fabrics A and B
- ¼ yd. (23cm) each of two different red prints for fabrics C and D
- ⅛ yd. (11cm) light green print for inner border
- 1 yd. (.9m) floral print for setting triangles, outer border and binding

- 21" × 58" (53cm x 147cm) rectangle of batting
- 1¼ yd. (1.1m) fabric for backing
- Paper-backed fusible web
- Thread to match fabrics A, B, C and D

FINISHED TABLE RUNNER: 18½" × 55"
  (47CM X 140CM)
FINISHED BLOCK SIZE: 8" (20CM)
NUMBER OF BLOCKS: 4
TEMPLATES NEEDED: TWIRLY BIRD CIRCLE SHAPE
  (TEMPLATE 1)

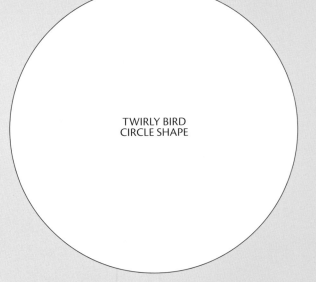

TWIRLY BIRD
CIRCLE SHAPE

Make this quick and easy runner to dress up a table in any room. Select a beautiful floral or large-print fabric first, and then pull four colors out to use for your "twirly bird" petals. This simple little block works perfectly with the Appli-Curves method.

Your finished runner has scrappy blocks, with one quarter of each complete circle used for the pinwheels. The corners of the curves are purposely short on one edge; this creates the illusion that the curve and the triangle join together.

Cut the Fabrics

To begin the Twirly Bird Table Runner, cut:

- Four 5½" (14cm) squares from white
- Eight 2⅞" (7cm) squares from white; sub-cut once on the diagonal to yield 16 triangles
- Sixteen 2½" × 4½" (6cm × 11cm) rectangles from white
- One 5" (13cm) square each from fabrics A, B, C and D
- Two 2⅞" (7cm) squares each from fabrics A, B, C and D; sub-cut once on the diagonal to yield four triangles each
- Three 1" (3cm) strips from the light-green print for the inner border
- Two 13" (33cm) squares from the floral print; sub-cut twice on the diagonal to yield eight setting triangles (six will be used)
- Four 3" (8cm) strips from the floral print for the outer borders
- Four 2¼" (6cm) strips from the floral print for the binding

Make the Center Patches

See Chapter 2 for basic block construction.

1 Print Template 1 from the CD. Trace four circle shapes onto the paper side of the fusible web, leaving at least ½" (1cm) between the shapes.

2 Cut out each circle, leaving approximately ¼" (6mm) extra outside of the pencil line. Trim the paper inside of the circle, approximately ¼" (6mm) away from the pencil line.

3 Fuse one circle onto the back of each 5" (13cm) fabric A, B, C and D square. Cut out each circle on the pencil line. Remove the paper backing.

4 Center, then fuse each circle shape onto the right side of each 5½" (14cm) white square. (The right sides of both fabrics will face up.) Matching the thread to the fabrics, machine-stitch around each circle. Trim the white behind the circle to approximately ¼" (6mm).

5 Using a transparent ruler and rotary cutter, trim each patch to 5" (13cm) square, making sure the circle is perfectly centered.

6 Using a transparent ruler and rotary cutter, cut each patch in half twice to yield four squares.

tip

I like to use the small zigzag stitch on this project so the stitching on the curve is as invisible as possible. Since I was trying to create the illusion that the quarter circle and the adjoining triangle are one object (the petal), I didn't want to draw any attention to my stitching on the curves.

Assemble the Blocks

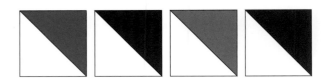

1 Join one 2⅞" (7cm) white triangle to each of the 2⅞" (7cm) fabric A, B, C and D triangles. You will have a total of 16 (four sets of four).

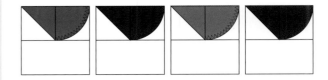

2 Sew the triangle patches to the matching square patches, as shown.

3 Sew one 2½" × 4½" (6cm × 11cm) white rectangle on each rectangle completed in step 2, as shown.

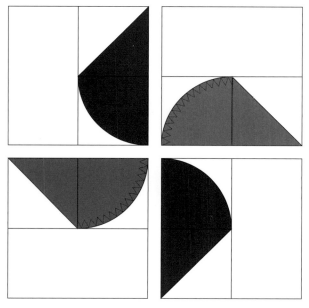

4 Lay out four of the patches completed in the previous step, one from each of fabrics A, B, C and D.

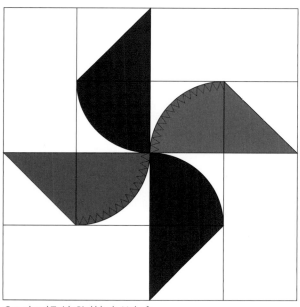

Completed Twirly Bird block. Make four.

5 Join the four patches to complete one block. Repeat steps 1–4 to create a total of four blocks.

Add the Setting Triangles

1 Lay out the blocks and the floral triangles as shown.

Rows 1–4.

2 Sew the blocks and floral triangles into four diagonal rows as shown in the diagram. Join each row to complete the center of the table runner. Press.

3 Examine your floral setting triangles. They were cut a little larger to accommodate individual variations in piecing and probably need trimming. Using a transparent ruler and rotary cutter, trim the floral triangles, leaving ¼" (6mm) seam allowances on both sides.

49

Add the Borders

Trim green print after stitching.

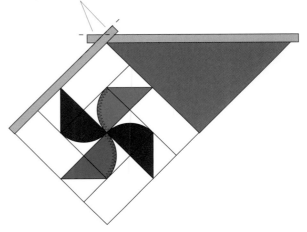

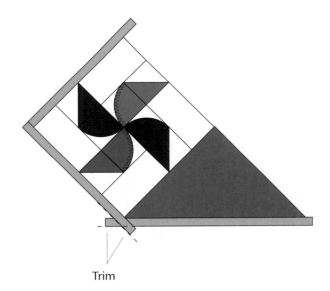

1 Center and sew one 1" (3cm) light-green strip to each long side of the table runner, being careful not to stretch the runner. The strips will extend past the edges of the table runner. Trim so ½" (1cm) of light-green remains on ends. Press the seam allowances toward the light-green strip.

2 Piece the remaining 1" (3cm) wide strip and scraps end-to-end with a diagonal seam to obtain a strip at least 44" (112cm) long. Sub-cut into four 11" strips (28cm). Sew one 11" (28cm) strip to each diagonal opposite end, stitching across the side strip. Press the seam allowances toward the light-green strip. Trim as shown.

Trim

3 Attach the remaining 11" (28cm) light-green strips to each remaining opposite corner end, stitching across the extended 1" (3cm) strips and corner at the point. Trim and press the seam allowances toward the light-green strip.

4 From the four 3" (8cm) floral strips, sub-cut two 3" × 15" (8cm × 38cm), two 3" × 18" (8cm × 46cm), and two 3" × 36" (8cm × 91cm) floral strips.

5 Center and sew the 3" × 36" (8cm × 91cm) floral strips to each long side of the table runner as you did for the light-green inner border. Add the 3" × 15" (8cm × 38cm) segments to each opposite end, and then attach the 3" × 18" (8cm × 46cm) segments to complete the table runner top. Press all seam allowances toward the inner border, and trim as needed.

Finish the Table Runner

1 Cut two 22" × 29½" (56cm × 75cm) rectangles from the backing fabric. Sew the two rectangles together on the 22' (56cm) edges so the finished rectangle measures 22' × 58½" (56cm × 149cm).

2 Layer, baste and quilt as desired.

3 Sew the 2¼" (6cm) floral strips together end-to-end with a diagonal seam. Fold the strip lengthwise, wrong sides together, and press to create the binding. Bind the table runner.

scarlet sunset throw

MATERIALS

- ¼ yd. or 9" (23cm) square black multicolored fabric
- ⅓ yd. (30cm) bright red fabric
- ½ yd. (46cm) cream print
- ½ yd. (46cm) bright orange fabric
- ½ yd. (46cm) black-and-red multicolored fabric
- ½ yd. (46cm) black print
- ½ yd. (46cm) deep red fabric
- ½ yd. (46cm) black-and-white print
- ½ yd. (46cm) black print for border and binding
- ½ yd. (46cm) multicolored print for border
- 45" × 54" (114cm x 137cm) rectangle of batting
- 1⅔ yd. (1.5m) fabric for backing
- Paper-backed fusible web
- Threads to match fabrics

FINISHED QUILT: 42" × 50" (107CM X 127CM)
FINISHED BLOCK SIZE: 4¼" (11CM)
UNFINISHED BLOCK SIZE: 4¾" (12CM)
NUMBER OF BLOCKS: 80
TEMPLATE NEEDED: DRUNKARD'S PATH CIRCLE SHAPE (TEMPLATE 2)

DRUNKARD'S PATH
CIRCLE SHAPE

This stunning setting is often seen on Log Cabin quilts, but the Drunkard's Path blocks require much less stitching. Great as a two-color quilt, or with fabrics repeating every few rounds, this arrangement can be adapted for any decor. The warm, rich colors remind me of the beautiful sunsets we occasionally see for a moment—but only if we are in the right place at the right time, slowing down enough to notice. Scarlet Sunset is the perfect size for a sofa throw, but you can add more rows and expand the size for any bed in your home.

Cut the Fabrics

To make the Scarlet Sunset Throw, cut:

- One 9½" (24cm) square from bright red
- Three 9½" (24cm) squares from cream print
- Three 9½" (24cm) squares from bright orange
- Four 9½" (24cm) squares from black-and-red multicolored
- Four 9½" (24cm) squares from black print

- Three 9½" (24cm) squares from deep red
- Two 9½" (24cm) squares from black-and-white print
- Four 1¼" (3cm) strips from black print for border
- Five 2¼" (6cm) strips from black print for binding
- Five 3½" (9cm) strips from multicolored print for border

Make the Blocks

See Chapter 2 for basic block construction.

1 Print Template 2 from the CD. Trace 20 Drunkard's Path circle shapes onto the paper side of the fusible web, leaving at least ½" (1cm) between the circles.

2 Cut out each circle approximately ¼" (6mm) outside the tracing lines. Trim away the inside of each paper circle, leaving about ¼" (6mm) on the inside of the tracing line.

3 Being careful not to distort the circle shapes, fuse the paper "rings" onto the wrong side of the following fabrics:

- 1 on black multicolored
- 2 on bright red
- 3 on cream
- 4 on bright orange
- 4 on black-and-red multicolored
- 3 on black print
- 2 on deep red
- 1 on black-and-white

4 Cut out the circles on the tracing line, cutting through both fabric and paper. Peel the paper backing from the fusible web.

5 Fuse the circles onto the centers of the 9½" (24cm) squares:

- Black multicolored circle onto the bright red square
- Bright red circles onto the cream squares (one cream square will be left over)
- Cream circles onto the bright orange squares

- Bright orange circles onto the black-and-red multicolored squares
- Black-and-red multicolored circles onto the black squares
- Black circles onto the deep red squares
- Deep red circles onto the black-and-white squares
- Black-and-white circle onto the remaining cream square

6 Using thread to match the circle fabric, stitch around the curved edge on each patch.

7 Cut twice through the center of each piece. Your blocks will be 4¾" (12cm).

tip

Finding quilting designs to work in the open areas can be a challenge if you try to base your design on the block. Instead, view the bands of color as a border, and look for simple 2"–3" (5cm–8cm) border designs.

The bands of color make the perfect space to quilt a design. Check your border stencils for ideas on what might work best.

Assemble the Quilt

1 Arrange the blocks according to the diagram.

2 Join the blocks in each row, pressing seam allowances in opposite directions for each row.

3 Join the rows, butting the seam allowances between the blocks. Press all seam allowances to one side.

> ### tip
>
> *Pressing the seam allowances open might allow the batting to "beard" through the tiny openings in the fabric between the stitches. That is why in quilting, whenever possible, you should press the seams to one side.*

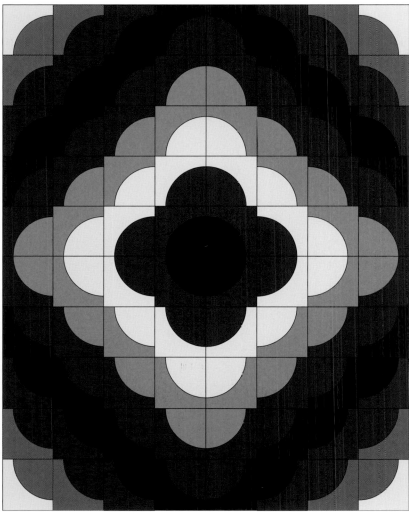

Quilt diagram.

Add the Borders

1 Join the 1¼" (3cm) black strips end-to-end with a diagonal seam.

2 Sub-cut the black borders into two 1¼" × 43" (3cm × 109cm) strips (for sides) and two 1¼" × 36' (3cm × 91cm) strips (for the top and bottom).

3 Fold the 1¼" × 43" (3cm × 109cm) black strips in half, and mark the center with a pin. Pin to the sides of the quilt, matching the centers. Pin the

borders at least every 4"–6" (10cm to 15cm). Stitch. Press. Attach the top and bottom black borders in the same manner.

4 Join the 3½" (9cm) multicolored strips end-to-end with a straight seam. Use straight seams on wider borders, as this reduces "waviness."

5 Sub-cut the multicolored strips into two 3½" × 44½" (9cm × 113cm) strips for the sides and two 3½" × 42" (9cm × 107cm) strips for the top and bottom.

6 Sew the outer borders the same way you sewed the inner borders.

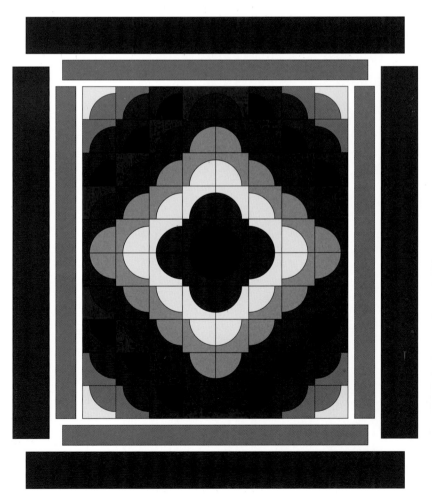

Add side borders, then the top and bottom.

Finish the Quilt

1 Mark the quilt top for quilting, using fabric-marking pencils.

2 Remove the selvages from the backing fabric, and piece to form a 45" × 54" (114cm × 137cm) rectangle. Press.

3 Layer, baste and quilt as desired.

4 Trim the excess batting and backing even with the edges of the quilt top.

5 Diagonally piece 2¼" (6cm) binding fabric strips to create one continuous strip of binding. Press wrong sides together, then attach and turn to bind the quilt.

6 Make a label for your quilt listing your name, address, date of completion and any other information you choose. You will be glad you did!

Finished quilt top.

barn raising framed art

MATERIALS

- 4" (10cm) square of white-and-pink print for the center
- 7" (18cm) square of pink print
- 7" × 24" (18cm x 61cm) rectangle of floral print
- 7" × 26" (18cm x 66cm) rectangle of cream print
- 7" × 16" (18cm x 41cm) rectangle of red print
- ⅓ yd. (30cm) black print

- Paper-backed fusible web
- Black thread for appliqué
- Permanent spray adhesive
- 16" (41cm) cream mat board with 12" × 12" (30cm x 30cm) opening
- 16" × 16" (41cm x 41cm) black picture frame and framing board

FINISHED FRAMED PROJECT: 16" (41CM) SQUARE
FINISHED UNFRAMED QUILT: 12" (30CM) SQUARE
UNFINISHED BLOCK SIZE: 2½" (6CM) SQUARE
FINISHED BLOCK SIZE: 2" (5CM) SQUARE
NUMBER OF BLOCKS: 36
TEMPLATES NEEDED: DRUNKARD'S PATH
    MINIATURE CIRCLE SHAPE (TEMPLATE 3)
    AND FRAMED ART LEAF SHAPE (TEMPLATE 4)

DRUNKARD'S PATH
MINIATURE CIRCLE SHAPE

FRAMED ART
LEAF SHAPE

These snippets of old fabrics from my stash were calling out to me because the colors were so pleasing. Pinks and blacks combine to create a color scheme I would not usually choose. Instead of the traditional fabric border, I decided to use an art mat and frame. My local hobby store framed the work for a very reasonable price. Adding the fabric leaves to the mat was the perfect accent to join the patchwork with the art frame and mat.

Cut the Fabrics

To begin the Barn Raising Framed Art, cut:

- Two 6" (15cm) squares from pink
- Two 6" (15cm) squares from floral
- Three 6" (15cm) squares from cream
- Two 6" (15cm) squares from red
- One 6" (15cm) square from black
- Two 3½" × 12½" (9cm × 32cm) rectangles from black
- Two 3½" × 18½" (9cm × 47cm) rectangles from black

Make the Blocks

See Chapter 2 for basic block construction.

1 Print Template 3 from the CD. Trace nine miniature circle shapes onto the paper side of the fusible web, leaving at least ½" (1cm) between the circles.

2 Cut out each paper circle, leaving approximately ¼" (6mm) extra outside the tracing lines. Trim away the inside of each paper circle, leaving about ¼" (6mm) on the inside of the tracing line.

3 Being careful not to distort the circle shapes, fuse the paper "rings" onto the wrong side of your fabric. Fuse one to the center print, two to the pink, three to the floral, two to the cream and one to the red.

4 Cut out the circles on the tracing line, cutting through both fabric and paper. Peel the paper backing from the fusible web.

5 Fuse the circles onto the centers of the 6" (15cm) squares. Fuse one center print circle onto the pink square, two pink circles onto the floral squares, three floral circles onto the cream squares, two cream circles onto the red squares and one red circle onto the black square.

6 Cut twice through the center of each block. You will complete the stitching around the curves later in this project.

7 Using a transparent ruler, square up each block to 2½" (6cm). Make sure the curve is even on each block.

tip

Since the miniature quilt will be framed, stitching around the curves isn't necessary. This can be a real time-saver for last-minute gifts. Because of the small patches and the multicolored fabrics, I decided to use a solid black thread for the edge finishing. This worked to define the patches with a common outline and bring unity to the piece.

Buttonhole stitching gives a pleasing appearance.

Assemble the Art

1 Arrange the blocks as shown.

2 Join the blocks in each row, pressing the seam allowances in opposite directions for each row.

3 Join the rows, butting seam allowances between the blocks. Press all seam allowances to one side.

4 Using black thread and any decorative stitch you desire, stitch around each band of colored fabric that was created when the blocks were pieced.

> **tip**
>
> *Since this is a miniature, it is quicker and more efficient to do the stitching after the quilt top is complete. Since the patches are so small, the threads are more secure when stitched this way.*

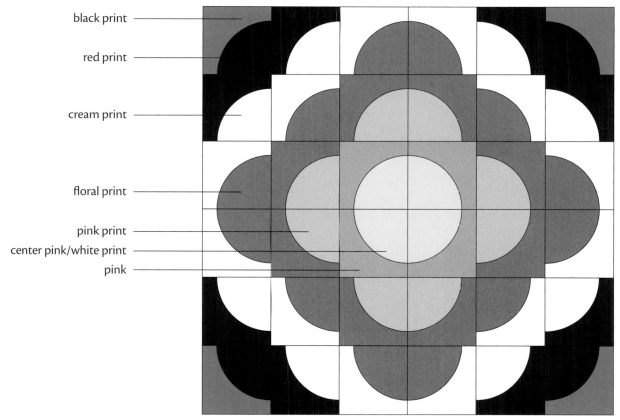

black print

red print

cream print

floral print

pink print

center pink/white print

pink

Block arrangement.

Finish the Project

1 Print Template 4 from the CD. Trace twelve leaf shapes onto the paper side of the fusible web, leaving about ½" (1cm) of space between the shapes. Fuse onto the back of the black print.

2 Cut out the shapes on the pencil line. Remove the paper from the fusible web.

3 Fuse four leaf shapes onto the center of the quilt, matching the ends of the leaves in the center. Stitch the leaves in place using a very small zigzag, crossing the stitching in the center of the leaves to avoid stopping and starting.

4 Attach the 3½" × 12½" (9cm × 32cm) black rectangles to the opposite sides of the quilt. Add the 3½" × 18½" (9cm × 47cm) black rectangles to the remaining sides. This border will not show when the quilt is framed, but it will be needed to stretch the quilt over the framing board.

5 Stretch the quilt over the framing board, and tape the edges down on the back. Add a cream mat and black frame.

6 Using spray adhesive, glue the remaining black leaves to the mat board.

Finished quilt top.

Center leaves stitched in place.

Black leaves glued to the mat board.

cabana throw

Finished quilt: 45" × 101" (114cm x 257cm)
Finished block: 4¼" (11cm)
Unfinished block: 4¾" (12cm)
Number of blocks: 45
Templates needed: Drunkard's Path Circle Shape (Template 2), Cabana Large Flower (Template 5), Cabana Medium Flower (Template 6), Cabana Small Flower (Template 7), Cabana Small Leaf (Template 8) and Cabana Large Leaf (Template 9)

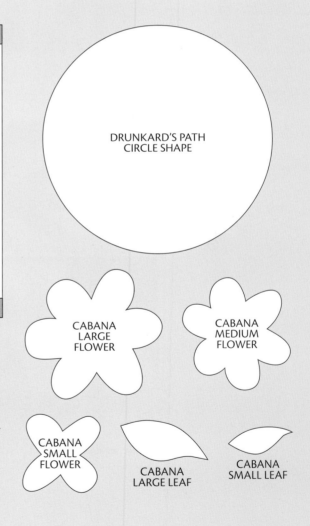

This throw is super-fast using the Appli-Curves technique. A decorative stitch and variegated thread was used to add interest and add to the quilt's whimsy. The quick blocks are set in vertical rows, which seemed to demand appliqué. The flower shapes were inspired by the fabrics used for the blocks, but the shapes alone will complement any fabric choice. This cheery quilt will brighten a room with lots of color, or make the perfect throw or lap quilt.

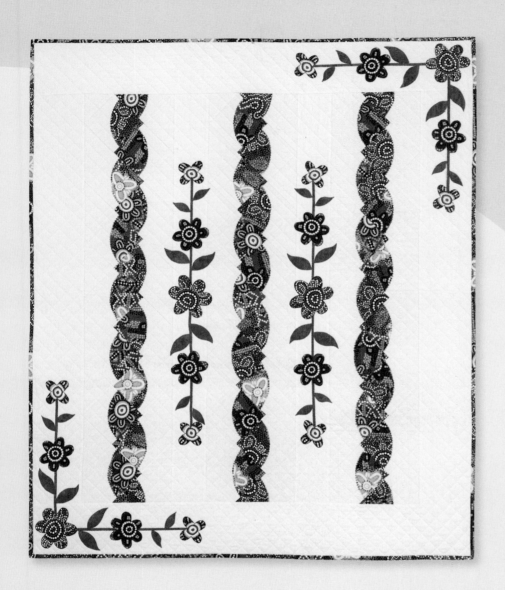

Cut the Fabrics

To begin the Cabana Throw, cut:

- Three 9½" (24cm) strips from white; sub-cut into twelve 9½" (24cm) squares
- Two 7¼" (18cm) strips from white; sub-cut into ten 7¼" (18cm) squares; sub-cut twice on the diagonal to yield 40 triangles (you'll only use 39)

- One 3⅞" (10cm) strip from white; sub-cut into three 3⅞" (10cm) squares; sub-cut once on the diagonal to yield six triangles
- Five 4" (10cm) strips from white
- Seven 6" (15cm) strips from white for the borders
- Eight 2¼" (6cm) strips from multicolored for the binding

If fabrics are multicolored, a variegated thread is often the best choice for finishing the edges of the Drunkard's Path curves. Even though the same fabrics were used for both the appliqué flowers and the blocks, the flowers seemed to call for more definition, so a solid thread was used to finish the edge.

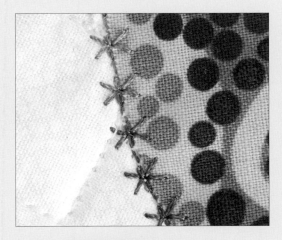

Make the Blocks

See Chapter 2 for basic block construction.

1 Print Template 2 from the CD. Trace 12 circle shapes onto the paper side of the fusible web, leaving at least ½" (1cm) extra between the circles.

2 Cut out each paper circle approximately ¼" (6mm) outside of the tracing lines. Trim away the inside of each paper circle, leaving about ¼" (6mm) on the inside of the tracing line. (See the dotted line inside the circle shape.)

3 Being careful not to distort the circle shapes, fuse the paper "rings" onto the wrong side of the multicolored fabric.

4 Cut out the circles on the tracing line, cutting through both fabric and paper. Peel the paper backing from the fusible web. Fuse the circles onto the exact centers of the 9½" (24cm) white squares.

5 Stitch around the curved edge of the circle fabric on each patch. Use the blanket stitch, zigzag stitch or any decorative stitch you choose.

6 Cut twice through the center of each block, to create a total of 48 blocks. Your finished patches will be 4¾" (12cm).

Make the Quilt Center

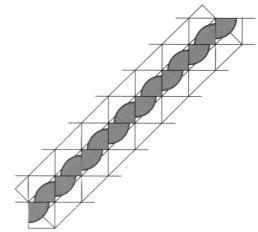

Piecing diagram for the block strip.

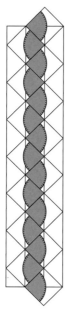

Row layout.

1 Lay out 15 blocks, 13 large white triangles and two small white triangles to complete a vertical row. (The end blocks will extend and be trimmed later.)

2 Put the two small white triangles aside for now. Piece each diagonal row, beginning with Row 1. Add one small white triangle to the top of Row 1 and to the end of Row 7. Join the rows to complete the block strip.

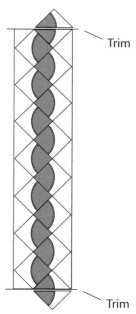

Trim

Trim

Square up the block strips.

3 Repeat steps 1 and 2 to complete a total of three block strips. Using a rotary cutter and transparent ruler, trim the blocks at the top and bottom of the block strips at a 45-degree angle.

4 Piece the 4" (10cm) white strips end-to-end with a diagonal seam. Sub-cut into two 4" × 90½" (10cm × 230cm) strips.

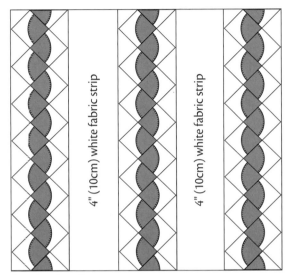

Complete the quilt center.

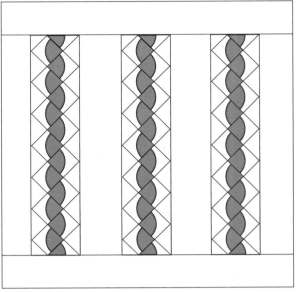

Completed quilt top.

8 Sew the 6" × 45½" (15cm × 116cm) strips to the top and bottom of the patchwork.

5 Attach the white strips between the block rows.

6 Piece the 6" (15cm) white strips end-to-end with a diagonal seam. Sub-cut into two 6" × 90½" (15cm × 230cm) strips and two 6" × 45½" (15cm × 116cm) strips.

7 Sew the 6" × 90½" (15cm × 230cm) strips to the sides of the patchwork.

Add the Appliqué

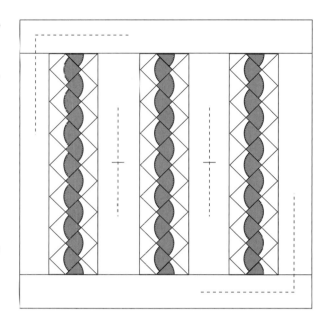

1 To make green stems, fuse a 4½" × 6' (11cm × 15cm) rectangle of fusible web onto the wrong side of the green. Using a rotary cutter and transparent ruler, sub-cut into 16¼" × 6" segments (41cm × 15cm). Remove the paper backing.

2 Print templates 5–9 from the CD. Trace the appliqué shapes onto the paper side of your fusible web, leaving ½" (1cm) between the pencil lines. Trace four Cabana Large Flowers, eight Cabana Medium Flowers, eight Cabana Small Flowers, 16 Cabana Small Leaf Shapes and 16 Cabana Large Leaf Shapes.

3 As you did for the circle shapes, trim the middles from each paper shape, leaving about ¼" (6mm) of paper inside the tracing lines.

4 Fuse the tracings onto the wrong side of the fabrics. Fuse:

- 4 Cabana Large Flowers onto the multicolored
- 8 Cabana Medium Flowers onto the multicolored
- 8 Cabana Small Flowers onto the multicolored
- 16 Cabana Small Leaf Shapes onto the green
- 16 Cabana Large Leaf Shapes onto the green

5 Cut out the shapes on the pencil lines, cutting through both the paper and fabrics. Peel the paper backing from the fusible web.

6 Using a fabric marking pencil or chalk, mark the center of the white strips between the block rows and the opposite corners on the borders.

tip

If your fabric does not lend itself to "broderie purse" (cutting shapes from the multicolored fabric), substitute other fabrics for the flowers and create a small circle shape for the flower centers, if needed.

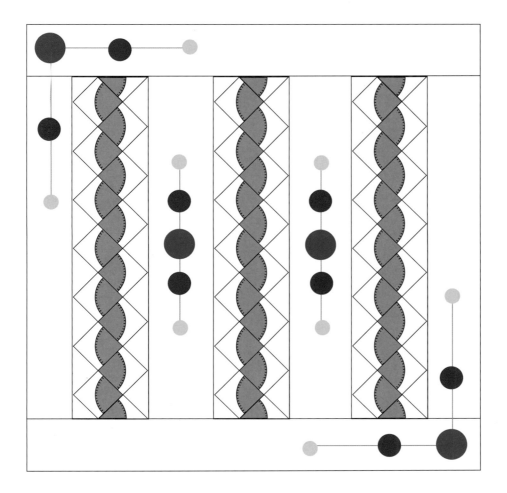

7 Arrange the shapes between the block rows and
on the opposite corners as shown, using the markings to help keep the stems straight. Trim stems if they
are too long, and tuck the stem ends under the flowers.
Fuse the shapes in place.

8 Using thread to match the fabrics, stitch around
the curved edges of the shapes on each patch.
Use the blanket stitch, zigzag stitch or any other decorative stitch.

Finish the Throw

1 Mark the top for quilting, using fabric-marking pencils.

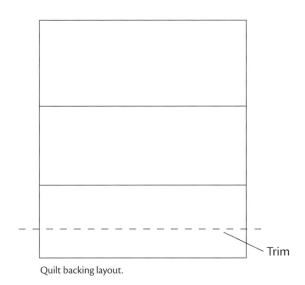

Quilt backing layout.

2 Remove the selvages from the backing fabric. Cut the backing into three 50" (127cm) sections, and then piece as shown. Trim the bottom section so the backing measures 50" × 106" (127cm × 269cm). Press.

3 Layer, baste and quilt as desired.

4 Trim excess batting and backing even with the edges of the quilt.

5 Diagonally piece the 2¼" (6cm) binding fabric strips to make one continuous strip of binding. Press wrong sides together, then attach and turn to bind the quilt.

6 Add a quilt label.

tip

With so much open space, I decided to have a grid design quilted into the background. First, stitch "in the ditch" around the appliqué and the curved edges, and then fill in with the 45-degree grid.

Quilt detail.

71

harvest bloom table runner

MATERIALS

- ⅓ yd. (30cm) each gold 1, gold 2 and rust fabrics
- 1⅛ yd. (1m) dark green fabric
- ⅔ yd. (60cm) or fat quarter cranberry fabric
- ⅛ yd. (11cm) yellow fabric
- 24" × 56" (61cm x 142cm) rectangle of batting
- 1⅓ yd. (1.2m) fabric for backing
- Paper-backed fusible web

FINISHED TABLE RUNNER: 20" × 52" (51CM X 132CM)

FINISHED BLOCK SIZE: 11¾" (30CM)

UNFINISHED BLOCK SIZE: 12¼" (31CM)

NUMBER OF BLOCKS: 3

TEMPLATES NEEDED: DRUNKARD'S PATH CIRCLE SHAPE (TEMPLATE 2), HARVEST BLOOM FLOWER (TEMPLATE 10), HARVEST BLOOM FLOWER CENTER (TEMPLATE 11) AND HARVEST BLOOM LEAF (TEMPLATE 12)

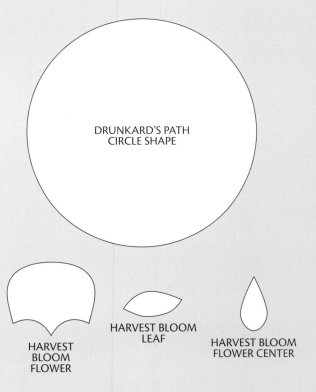

DRUNKARD'S PATH CIRCLE SHAPE

HARVEST BLOOM FLOWER

HARVEST BLOOM LEAF

HARVEST BLOOM FLOWER CENTER

Look closely at a Spiced Pinks block, and you'll see it is really just a Drunkard's Path with flower appliqué. In the past, the combination of curved piecing and hand appliqué may have discouraged you from even considering this beauty in your projects. With fusible web methods, this table runner can be stitched in a fraction of the time! Adding angled ends to this project is another easy way to create more interest.

Cut the Fabrics

To begin the Harvest Bloom Table Runner, cut:

- One 9½" (24cm) square each from gold 1, gold 2 and rust; sub-cut each square once on the diagonal to yield four triangles
- Two 7¼" (18cm) squares each from gold 1, gold 2 and rust; sub-cut each square once on the diagonal to yield four triangles
- One 5" × 12¼" (13cm × 31cm) rectangle each from gold 1 and gold 2
- Two 9" × 12¼" (23cm × 31cm) rectangles from dark green
- Three 8" (20cm) squares from dark green
- Three 3¾" (10cm) strips from dark green for the border
- Four 2¼" (6cm) strips from dark green for the binding
- Four 1¼" (3cm) cranberry strips for the inner border
- One 24" × 56" (61cm × 142cm) rectangle from the backing

This project uses an adaptation of the Spiced Pinks block found in *501 Quilt Blocks: Treasury of Patterns for Patchwork & Appliqué* (Better Homes and Gardens, 1994).

Make the Blocks

See Chapter 2 for basic block construction.

1 Print Template 2 from the CD. Trace three circle shapes onto the paper side of fusible web. Cut the fusible web, leaving ½" (1cm) outside the tracing lines.

2 Trim inside each paper circle by cutting approximately ¼" (6mm) from the circle tracing line. Fuse the circles onto the wrong side of the 8" (20cm) dark green squares, being careful not to distort the circles.

3 Cut out the circles on the tracing lines, cutting through both the fabric and the paper. Peel the paper backing from the fusible web.

4 Fold the dark green circles equally into fourths, and pierce the centers with a straight pin. Fold the 9½" (24cm) gold 1, gold 2 and rust squares equally into fourths, and pierce the centers with a straight pin.

5 Using a straight pin to line up the centers (the pin should be perpendicular to the fabrics), fuse the circles onto the centers of the gold 1, gold 2 and rust squares.

6 Stitch around the circle on each square, matching the thread to the dark green.

7 Using a rotary cutter and transparent ruler, cut twice through the center of each block to create four Drunkard's Path blocks.

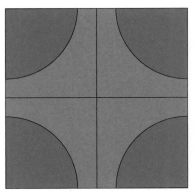

Complete the block center. Make three.

8 Arrange each Drunkard's Path block as shown, and piece to complete the block center.

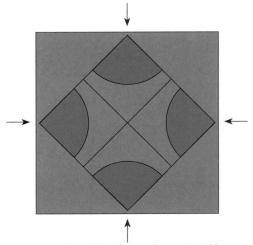

Be sure the ¼" (6mm) seam allowance is visible beyond the points (see arrows).

9 Add the 7¼" (18cm) triangles to each corner of the block center blocks.

10 Square up the blocks to 12¼" (31cm), making sure the ¼" (6mm) seam allowance remains on all four edges.

Add the Appliqué Blossoms

Place the appliqué.

1 Print templates 10–12 from the CD. Trace the flower, flower center and leaf shapes onto the paper side of the fusible web, leaving ½" (1cm) between the pencil lines. Trace 14 Harvest Bloom Flowers on cranberry, 14 Harvest Bloom Flower Centers on yellow and 28 Harvest Bloom Leaves on dark green.

2 As you did for the circle shapes, trim the middles from each paper shape, leaving about ¼" (6mm) of paper inside the tracing lines.

3 Fuse the tracings onto the wrong side of the fabrics indicated in step 1.

4 Cut out the shapes on the pencil lines, cutting through both the paper and the fabric. Peel the paper backing from the fusible web.

5 To make dark green stems, fuse a 1½" × 8" (4cm × 20cm) rectangle of fusible web onto the wrong side of the dark green. Using a rotary cutter and transparent ruler, sub-cut into fourteen ½" × 1" (1cm × 3cm) segments.

6 Arrange the shapes on each block according to the drawing shown. The stems should sit just on the seam line and tuck under the flowers. Extra shapes will be used in a later section.

7 Following the manufacturer's instructions, fuse the shapes in place.

8 Using thread to match your fabrics, stitch around the curved edge of the shapes on each patch. Use the blanket stitch, zigzag stitch or any other decorative stitch you like.

tip

Changing the color scheme totally alters the look of your project. Because this table runner is quick and fun, it can be made to fit any decor, and makes the perfect gift.

Assemble the Table Runner

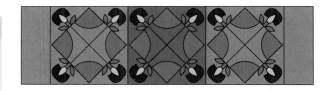

1 Sew the blocks and each 5" × 12¼" (13cm × 31cm) rectangle together as shown. Match the 5" × 12¼" (13cm × 31cm) gold 1 rectangle to the gold 1 block, and match the 5" × 12¼" (13cm × 31cm) gold 2 rectangle to the gold 2 block.

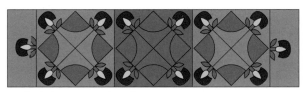

Appliqué placement on the ends.

2 Fuse the remaining flowers, leaves and stems onto the end rectangles.

3 Stitch to finish the edges of all shapes, matching thread colors to the shape colors.

Angle the Ends and Add Borders

1 Mark 2½" (6cm) from each corner on the rect-angle ends, as shown.

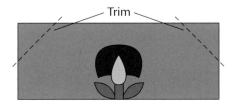

2 Draw a diagonal line between the two marks on each corner.

Angle the ends of the table runner.

3 Trim the rectangles on the lines.

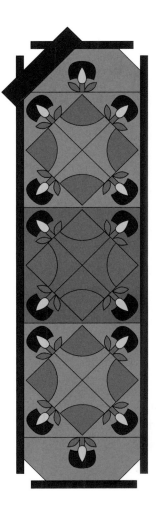

4 Join the 1¼" (3cm) cranberry strips end-to-end with a diagonal seam. Sub-cut into two 52" (132cm) and two 10" (25cm) segments.

5 Sew the 52" (132 cm) cranberry strips to the sides and the 10 segments to the top and bottom of the table runner, being careful not to stretch the patchwork as you stitch. Press.

6 Using leftover 1¼" (3cm) cranberry strips, attach segments to the angled ends, trimming off excess fabric underneath to finish the first border.

7 Join, then sew the 3¾" (10cm) dark green strips to the table runner the same way you attached the cranberry border. Trim all seams to ¼" (6mm). Press.

Finish the Table Runner

1 Mark the table runner top for quilting using fabric-marking pencils.

2 Remove the selvages from the backing fabric, and piece to form a 24" × 56" (61cm × 142cm) rectangle. Press.

3 Layer, baste and quilt as desired.

4 Trim excess batting and backing even with the edges of the table runner.

5 Piece the 2¼" (6cm) binding fabric strips on the diagonal to make one continuous strip of binding. Press wrong sides together, then attach and turn to bind the table runner.

Blanket stitching was used not only to finish the edges of the Drunkard's Path, but also to finish the raw-edge appliqué.

Completed table runner top.

HEARTS AND GIZZARDS:
TRADITIONAL BLOCK WITH A TWIST

This is my variation of the old-time Hearts and Gizzards block. I was fortunate to come across an antique two-color quilt of this name. I was intrigued with the positive-negative color placement and the simplicity of the block, yet how complicated the finished quilt appeared. I noticed how the original quilt maker had beautifully hand-pieced the blocks, and I decided that a similar look can be easily achieved with the Appli-Curves method. In this chapter, I've presented four great projects that use this ageless block as my inspiration. Simple and yet so stunning when worked up in the different fabrics and layouts, these projects are a delight to complete.

4

floral parade quilt

MATERIALS

- 2 yd. (1.8m) cream print
- 2 yd. (1.8m) lavender print
- 4⅛ yd. (3.8m) large floral print in lavender and yellow
- ⅔ yd. (61cm) light-green fabric
- 71" × 106" (180cm x 269cm) rectangle of batting
- 6 yd. (5.5m) fabric for backing
- ⅔ yd. (61cm) fabric for binding
- Paper-backed fusible web
- Threads to match fabrics

FINISHED QUILT SIZE: APPROXIMATELY 66½" × 102" (169CM × 259CM)

FINISHED BLOCK SIZE: 7⅞" (20CM)

UNFINISHED BLOCK SIZE: 8⅜" (21CM)

NUMBER OF BLOCKS: 30

TEMPLATE NEEDED: HEART SHAPE (TEMPLATE 13)

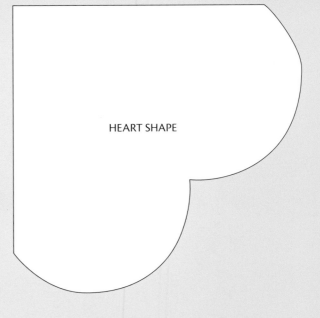

HEART SHAPE

Soft and pretty floral borders set off this vertical set of Hearts and Gizzards blocks. When choosing fabrics for this quilt, begin with the floral fabric. Then, pull two colors from the floral to use for the blocks. A soft green accent color was used as an inner border to contain the quilt center.

Cut the Fabrics

To begin the Floral Parade Quilt, cut:

- Four 8¾" (22cm) strips from cream; sub-cut into fifteen 8¾" (22cm) squares
- Four 8¾" (22cm) strips from lavender; sub-cut into fifteen 8¾" (22cm) squares

- Fourteen 10½" (27cm) strips from floral
- Two 10½" × 79¼" (27cm × 201cm) strips from floral
- Two 10½" × 71" (27cm × 180cm) strips from floral
- Two 10½" × 106" (27cm × 269cm) strips from floral
- Ten 2" (5cm) strips from light-green
- Nine 2¼" (6cm) strips for the binding

Prepare the Hearts

1 Print Template 13 from the CD. Trace 60 heart shapes onto the paper side of your fusible web, leaving at least 1" (3cm) between the hearts.

2 Cut out the shapes, leaving approximately ½" (1cm) outside of the pencil line.

3 Trim the paper inside of the shape to approximately ¼" (6mm) away from the pencil line.

Cut Out the Hearts

1 Fuse 30 hearts onto the back of the remaining cream fabric, and fuse 30 hearts onto the back of the remaining lavender fabric.

2 Cut out each heart on the pencil line, and remove the paper strips from the back of each shape.

Make the Blocks

See Chapter 2 for basic block construction.

 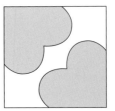

Make 15.   Make 15.

1 Fuse two cream hearts onto each lavender square and two lavender hearts onto each cream square, matching the sides and bottom of the shape to the opposite corners of the square (see page 29).

2 Using thread to match the fabric, stitch around the curved raw edges of the hearts.

3 On the back, trim away the background fabric so only about ¼"–½" (6mm–1cm) remains by the stitching. Using a rotary cutter and transparent ruler, cut the blocks once on the diagonal, cutting each heart in half.

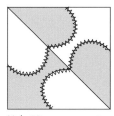

Make 30.

4 Re-arrange the half-blocks so a lavender background is paired with a cream background. Using
a ¼" (6mm) seam allowance, stitch a center seam on
each block to complete 30 blocks.

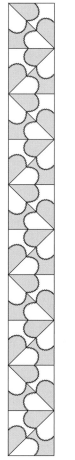

Make three of these rows.

5 Arrange 10 blocks in a row as shown. Make three
rows.

Final quilt layout. Mark the centers on the quilt edges in
preparation for mitering the borders.

- -

Assemble the Top

- -

1 Join the fourteen 10½" (27cm) floral strips
end-to-end on the diagonal. Sub-cut two 10½"
× 79¼" (27cm × 202cm) strips for the quilt center,
two 10½" × 71" (27cm × 180cm) strips for the outside
border, and two 10½" × 106" (27cm × 269cm) strips
for the outside border.

A light-green accent color was chosen for the inner border.

2 Join the 2" (5cm) light-green strips end-to-end with a diagonal seam.

3 Lay out the block strips and 79¼" (202cm) floral sections according to the diagram.

4 With a fabric-marking pencil, mark the center edge of the quilt on all sides.

5 Piece the light-green and floral border of the same length. Sew the 106" (269cm) border to the sides of the quilt, and sew the 71" (180cm) borders to the top and bottom, following the mitering instructions given on page 18.

6 Miter each corner. Press.

tip

The coloring on the border fabric required that the corners be mitered. Don't be intimidated—mitered corners are easier than they look, and the results are worth the extra effort. For instructions for mitering the borders, see page 18.

tip

I was lucky to find this lovely two-sided floral with lavender on one edge and yellow on the other. Originally, I planned a "spacer," or separator fabric, on each side of the Hearts and Gizzards blocks. However, the spacers actually took away from the beautiful border fabric. If you're unable to find a two-sided floral, any floral will work between the vertical rows. If your block rows need more separation, consider adding one or two spacers.

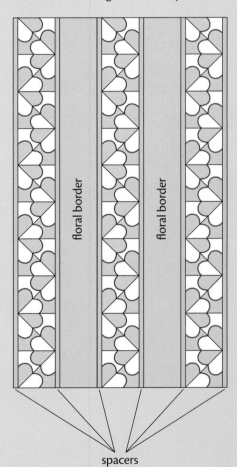

This was my original sketch of the quilt, before I omitted the spacers once the actual fabrics were placed.

Finish the Quilt

1 Using fabric-marking pencils, mark the top for quilting.

2 Remove the selvages from the backing fabric, and cut into two 40" × 106" (102cm × 269cm) rectangles. Seam as shown. Press.

3 Layer the quilt top, batting and backing. Baste and quilt.

4 Add binding and a quilt label.

Backing layout.

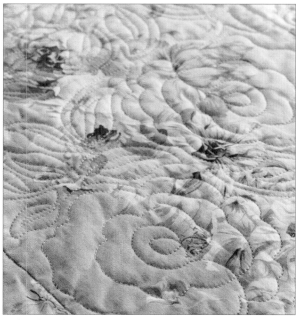

Quilt as desired.

tip

Using a stripe for bias binding is one of my favorite binding treatments. Although you'll need extra fabric, consider adding a stripe cut on the bias for this project.

You may choose to use a striped bias binding.

a cappella hearts quilt

MATERIALS

- ½ yd. (46cm) gold fabric
- 1⅔ yd. (1.5m) solid tan fabric
- 1½ yd. (1.4m) bright blue fabric
- ⅔ yd. (61cm) medium blue fabric
- 1⅛ yd. (1m) green fabric
- 3⅓ yd. (3m) ivory fabric
- 1⅓ yd. (1.2m) tan print
- ⅔ yd. (61cm) navy fabric
- 1⅓ yd. (1.2m) navy print

- 1½ yd. (1.4m) red fabric
- 4 yd. (3.7m) blue floral for border
- 92" × 108" (234cm x 274cm) rectangle of batting
- 7⅔ yd. (7m) fabric for backing
- 1 yd. (.9m) fabric for binding (on the bias)
- Paper-backed fusible web
- Thread to match fabrics
- Appliqué-pressing sheet

Finished quilt size: 88" × 104" (224cm x 264cm)

Finished block size: 15¾" (40cm)

Unfinished block size: 16¼" (41cm)

Number of blocks: 20

Templates needed: Heart Shape (Template 13) and Scallop Shape (Template 14)

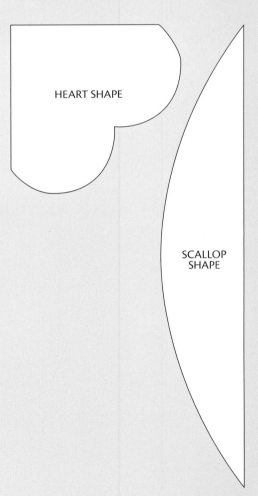

HEART SHAPE

SCALLOP SHAPE

This quilt combines many elements of traditional quilting: an old-time block, scrappy layout and a gorgeous scalloped border. The block design is carried into the top and bottom borders to add to the design interest. At first glance, these top and bottom borders may appear difficult to stitch, giving the illusion that they are pieced into both the borders. But, just as the blocks are constructed without curved piecing, the border treatment is as well. The half-blocks are fused over the borders and edge-stitched, making it a simple process with a big impact.

Cut the Fabrics

To create the A Cappella Hearts Quilt, cut:

- Four 8¾" (22cm) squares from gold
- Eighteen 8¾" (22cm) squares from ivory
- Ten 8¾" (22cm) squares from tan
- Ten 8¾" (22cm) squares from tan print
- Eight 8¾" (22cm) squares from bright blue
- Four 8¾" (22cm) squares from navy

- Four 8⅜" (22cm) squares from medium blue
- Eight 8¾" (22cm) squares from navy print
- Six 8¾" (22cm) squares from green
- Six 8¾" (22cm) squares from red
- Eight 1½" (4cm) strips for the inner borders from red
- Four 8¾" (22cm) squares from blue floral
- Nine 13" (33cm) strips from blue floral

Prepare the Hearts

1 Print Template 13 from the CD. Trace 160 hearts onto the paper side of the fusible web, leaving at least 1" (3cm) between the pencil lines.

2 Cut out the shapes, leaving approximately ½" (1cm) outside of the pencil line.

3 Trim the paper inside of the shape to approximately ⅛"–¼" (3mm–6mm) away from the pencil line.

Cut Out the Hearts

1 Fuse the hearts onto the back of the fabrics. Fuse:

- 8 on gold
- 36 on ivory
- 20 on tan
- 16 on tan print
- 16 on bright blue
- 8 on navy
- 8 on medium blue
- 16 navy print
- 12 on green
- 12 on red
- 8 on blue floral

2 Cut out each heart on the pencil line. Remove the paper strips from the back of each shape.

Make the Blocks

See Chapter 2 for basic block construction.

1 Using the chart below, fuse two same-colored hearts to the appropriate 8¾" (22cm) square.

8¾" (22cm) squares	Heart shapes
4 navy and 4 ivory	8 navy and 8 ivory
8 bright blue and 8 tan print	16 bright blue and 16 tan print
4 navy print and 4 ivory	8 navy print and 8 ivory
4 red and 4 tan	8 red and 8 tan
4 medium blue and 4 gold	8 medium blue and 8 gold
4 blue floral and 4 ivory	8 blue floral and 8 ivory
4 navy print and 4 tan	8 navy print and 8 tan
2 red and 2 ivory	4 red and 4 ivory
4 green and 4 ivory	8 green and 8 ivory
2 green and 2 tan	4 green and 4 tan

Row 1	Medium blue and gold	Busy navy and ivory	Red and tan	Bright blue and busy tan
Row 2	Green and tan	Bright blue and busy tan	Border and ivory	Green and ivory
Row 3	Red and ivory	Busy navy and tan	Navy and ivory	Busy navy and tan
Row 4	Bright blue and busy tan	Border and ivory	Medium blue and gold	Red and tan
Row 5	Busy navy and ivory	Green and ivory	Bright blue and busy tan	Navy and ivory

2 Using thread to match the fused heart fabric, stitch around the curved raw edges of the hearts.

3 On the back, trim away the background fabric so about ¼"–½" (6mm–1cm) remains by the stitching.

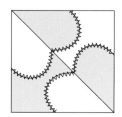

4 Using a rotary cutter and transparent ruler, cut the blocks once on the diagonal, bisecting the hearts. Rearrange the half-blocks so opposite colored halves are matched. Stitch with ¼" (6mm) seam allowances.

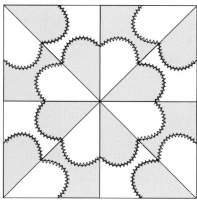

Completed block. Make 20 according to the chart.

5 Arrange four sections as shown to complete the block.

Assemble the Top

1 Lay out the blocks according to the chart and diagram above.

2 Join each row, then join the rows to complete the center. Press.

tip

There will be many fabric layers in the center of the blocks where the seams come together. To minimize this, consider pressing the seams in a clockwise spiral, or try pressing them open. Be careful when pressing the overall blocks; they will be thicker where the seams intersect, and they can become shiny with heat and extra pressure from the iron.

Add the Borders

1 Piece 1½" (4cm) red strips end-to-end with a diagonal seam. Sub-cut into two 1½" × 65¾" (4cm × 167cm) segments for the top and bottom, and two 1½" × 79½" (4cm × 202cm) segments for the sides.

2 Attach 79½" (202cm) segments to the sides of the quilt top. Attach the 65¾" (167cm) segments to the top and bottom.

3 Piece the 13" (33cm) border strips end-to-end with a straight seam. Sub-cut into two 13" × 81½" (33cm × 207cm) segments for the sides, and two 13" × 91¼" (33cm × 232cm) segments for the top and bottom.

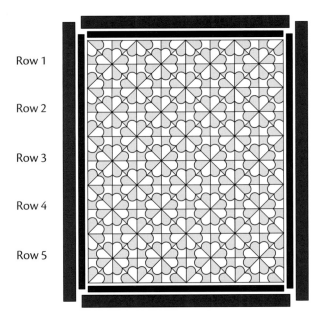

Row 1

Row 2

Row 3

Row 4

Row 5

4 Attach the 81½" (207cm) segments to the sides of the quilt top and the 91¼" (232cm) segments to the top and bottom.

tip

The border measurements are mathematically correct. Due to individual sewing differences, your actual measurements may vary slightly. Measure your quilt to verify.

1 Trace 24 additional hearts as you did for the block. Fuse 12 hearts onto the back of the bright blue and 12 onto the back of the ivory. **Cut out, but do not remove the paper backing.**

Do not remove paper backing.

2 Using a rotary cutter and transparent ruler, cut each shape down the center.

Make 24.

3 Using ¼" (6mm) seams, stitch to make 24 pairs of ivory and bright blue sets, as shown. You will be stitching through the paper of the fusible web. Finger press. (The paper will allow the patches to slide under the presser feet. If you removed the paper or it falls off, sandwich the seam between two strips of lightweight paper to keep it from sticking under the presser foot.)

Make 10 half moons.

4 Join 20 sets to make 10 half moons.

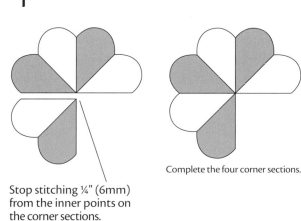

Stop stitching ¼" (6mm) from the inner points on the corner sections.

Complete the four corner sections.

5 To prepare the corner sections, stitch to a generous ¼" (6mm) from the points, and backstitch to knot. Remove all paper.

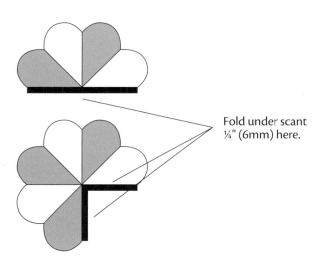

Fold under scant ¼" (6mm) here.

6 Carefully turn under ¼" (6mm) (to the wrong side) on the bottom edge of your half moons and corner sections. Press with an iron, using an appliqué-pressing sheet. Be careful—the fusible web is exposed.

7 Position so the center seams of the half moons and corner sections line up with seams between the blocks, and the folded edge of the half moons and corner sections covers the red border completely. Pin in place.

Appliqué these edges, covering the red border.

8 Using invisible machine appliqué with a nylon thread in the needle, or hand appliqué, stitch half moons and corner sections to the quilt, covering the red border.

9 Lay the quilt edges flat. Pin the half moons and corner sections onto borders. Fuse the tops of the half moons and corner sections.

10 Stitch the raw edges of the heart shapes the same way as you did for the blocks, matching threads to the appropriate fabrics and concealing knots at the beginning and end of stitching as much as possible.

Quilt the Top

To minimize distortion, quilt your quilt top before scalloping the edges.

1 Mark the top for quilting, using fabric-marking pencils.

Backing layout.

2 Remove the selvages from the backing fabric, and cut into three 40" × 92" (102cm × 234cm) rectangles (width of fabric is 92" [234cm]). Seam as shown. Press.

3 Layer the quilt top, batting and backing. Baste and quilt, quilting well into the 13" (33cm) borders (remember, you'll be trimming them in a scallop in the next section).

tip

As a beginner quilter, I shied away from scalloped borders. They looked so complicated, and I feared I wouldn't be able to create them evenly. I figured out the method presented here, which is nearly fail-proof.

Scallop the Edges

1 Using a fabric-marking pencil, draw lines 9½" (24cm) from the edge of the blocks (inside the edge of the red border) all around the quilt. Mark lines extending from the corners and middles of each block into the 13" (33cm) borders.

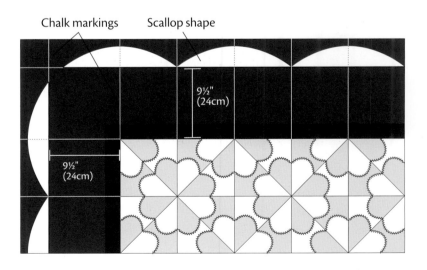

Chalk markings   Scallop shape

9½"
(24cm)

9½"
(24cm)

2 Print Template 14 from the CD. Trace the scallop shape onto heavy cardboard, like a file folder, and cut the shape out. Be sure to transfer the center marking on the cardboard shape.

3 Begin in the middle of a border. Position the flat edge of the scallop shape on the 9½" (24cm) line. Line up the center mark on the scallop with a line extending between the blocks. Line up the corners of the scallop with adjacent lines extending from the middles of the neighboring blocks. Once your position is correct, trace the top curve of the scallop with a fabric-marking pencil.

Join edges of scallops in the four corners.

4 Move the scallop to the left or right, and mark your next scallop. Work from the center of the borders out to the edges. If the shape does not match exactly, adjust as you mark. On the corners, you will have only the inner corners of the shape for reference. After all of the scallops are drawn, connect the edges of the corner scallops by hand with your marking pencil to complete the rounded corners, as shown.

tip

If you are using this quilt on the bed, you may want to leave the top border straight (not scalloped). This will help the quilt hang smoothly on your "made-up" bed.

5 Machine stitch ⅛" (3mm) inside the scallop markings to secure the edges before you cut. This will also assist you when applying the binding.

6 Cut the scalloped edges on the marking lines using scissors.

7 Make 400" (10.2m) of continuous 2½" (6cm) bias binding. It must be bias, so you can work it around the curves. Press wrong sides together, and then attach and turn to bind the quilt.

white cherries jubilee table topper

MATERIALS

- 2 yd. (1.8m) red print, including backing
- 1 yd. (.9m) white print
- ⅛ yd. (11cm) black print
- 29" × 29" (74cm x 74cm) square of batting
- Paper-backed fusible web
- Thread to match red and white fabrics

FINISHED SIZE: 29½" (75CM) DIAMETER
FINISHED BLOCK SIZE: 4⅛" (10CM)
UNFINISHED BLOCK SIZE: 4⅝" (12CM)
NUMBER OF FULL BLOCKS: 24
NUMBER OF HALF BLOCKS: 8
TEMPLATE NEEDED: MINIATURE HEART SHAPE
   (TEMPLATE 15)

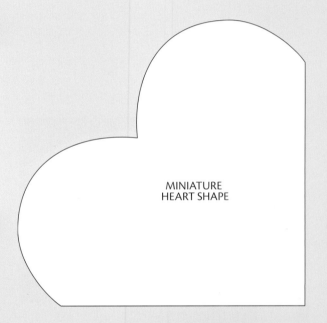

MINIATURE
HEART SHAPE

This snappy table topper is sure to draw an admirer's eye. Its interesting shape, petite patchwork and borders, and clean color scheme all play a part. Small and manageable, this is a great project for that special person—or for you! Choose just two colors, and then pick an accent for the tiny border.

Cut the Fabrics

To begin the White Cherries Jubilee Table Topper, cut:

- Two 5" (13cm) strips from red; sub-cut fourteen 5" (13cm) squares
- Two 5" (13cm) strips from white; sub-cut fourteen 5" (13cm) squares
- Three ⅞" (2cm) strips from black
- Four 2½" (6cm) strips from red

Prepare the Hearts

1 Print Template 15 from the CD. Trace 56 miniature heart shapes onto the paper side of the fusible web, leaving at least 1" (3cm) extra between the pencil lines.

2 Cut out the shapes, leaving approximately ½" (1cm) outside of the pencil line. Trim the paper inside of the shape to approximately ⅛"–¼" (3mm–6mm) away from the pencil line.

Cut Out the Hearts

1 Fuse 28 hearts onto the back of the remaining red fabric, and fuse 28 hearts onto the back of the remaining white fabric.

2 Cut out each heart on the pencil line. Remove the paper strips from the back of each shape.

Make the Blocks

See Chapter 2 for basic block construction.

Make 14.

Make 14.

1 Fuse two red hearts onto each white square. Place the hearts in the opposite corners of the square, matching the sides and bottom of the shapes to the corners of the square. Make 14. In the same way, fuse two white hearts to the opposite corners of a red square. Make 14.

2 Using thread to match the fused heart fabric, stitch around the curved raw edges of the hearts. Use a buttonhole, small zigzag or any decorative stitch for raw edge appliqué.

3 On the back, trim away the background fabric so about ¼"–½" (6mm–1cm) remains by stitching. Using a rotary cutter and transparent ruler, cut blocks once on the diagonal to bisect the hearts, as shown.

Make 24.

4 Rearrange the 48 half-blocks so a cut red background is paired with a white background. Using ¼" (6mm) seams, stitch a center seam to compete 24 blocks (you will have 8 half-blocks remaining: 4 red on white and 4 white on red).

5 Arrange 24 blocks and 8 half-blocks as shown.

6 Join each row, then join the rows to complete the quilt center. There is a lot of bulk where all seams come together in the center. Consider pressing seams in a clockwise spiral or try pressing them open. Press.

tip

Don't have a round table that this project will look great on? After I finished this "table topper," I laid it over the back of my recliner. It was the perfect accent for the room and fit the recliner like a glove! Later, the topper ended up over the back of our love seat in the front room and looked striking there, as well.

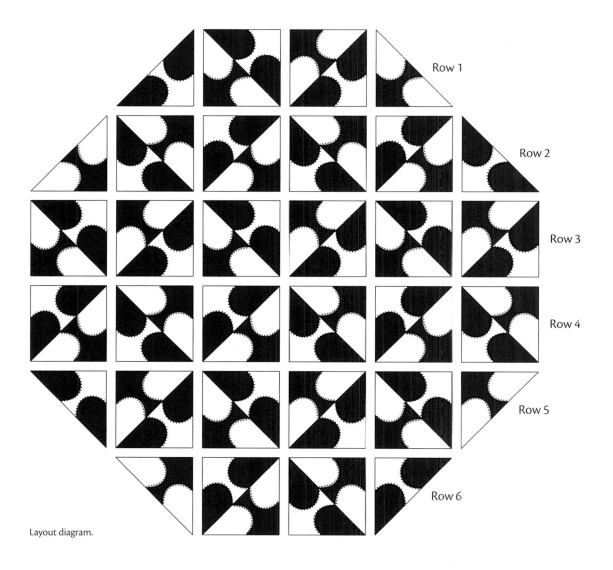

Row 1
Row 2
Row 3
Row 4
Row 5
Row 6

Layout diagram.

Add the Borders

1 Sew the ⅞" (2cm) black strips to the four edges shown, leaving about 1½" (4cm) of black border on the ends. Press the borders out, with seams toward the black.

2 Attach the ⅞" (2cm) black border to the remaining four edges, stitching across the borders applied in the previous step. Trim seams to ¼" (6mm) underneath the last-applied border. Press all borders out with seams toward the black.

Finished quilt top.

3 Add 2½" (6cm) red borders the same way as the black borders. Press.

Finish the Topper

1 Lay the 29" (74cm) batting square on table. Cover it with a 29" (74cm) red square, with the right side facing up.

2 Wrong side facing down, center the quilt top over the batting and 29" (74cm) square backing. Pin in place. Using ¼" (6mm) seam allowances, stitch around the entire topper, leaving an opening on one edge to turn.

3 Turn the topper so the right sides are facing out. Work the edges by seams so they are fully extended, and press. Tuck under ¼" (6mm) on the opening edges, and hand-stitch the opening shut.

4 Topstitch with matching thread, using a ¼" (6mm) seam allowance, all the way around the topper. Baste the center of your topper with safety pins. Quilt as desired.

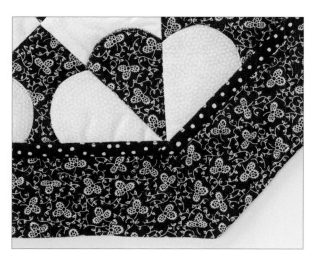

Topstitching ¼" (6mm) from the turned edge helps to stabilize the quilt and gives the appearance (at quick glance) of an applied binding. Use a walking foot and be careful not to stretch the edges as you stitch to obtain a flat finish.

Since this project uses smaller blocks, extensive quilting is not needed. On my sample, I quilted all the seams (including the curves and the narrow black border) "in the ditch." Then, I added a simple quilting design in the wide border.

cheese and crackers wall hanging

MATERIALS

- ½ yd. (46cm) red print
- ½ yd. (46cm) dark gold print
- ½ yd. (46cm) light gold print
- ½ yd. (46cm) green print
- 1⅓ yd. (1.2m) black print

- 36" × 36" (91cm x 91cm) square of batting
- 1 yd. (.9m) fabric for backing
- 1 yd. (.9m) fabric for binding
- Paper-backed fusible web
- Thread to match fabrics

FINISHED QUILT SIZE: 31½" (80CM) SQUARE
FINISHED BLOCK SIZE: 15¾" (40CM)
UNFINISHED BLOCK SIZE: 16¼" (41CM)
NUMBER OF BLOCKS: 4
TEMPLATE NEEDED: HEART SHAPE (TEMPLATE 13)

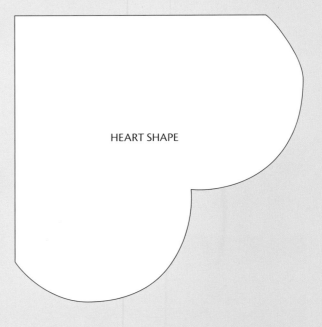

HEART SHAPE

Bold black fabric is the common element in all four blocks in this simple, small and quick project. When I teach my Hearts and Gizzards technique, this is often the project I choose. Perfect for a three-hour class, the Cheese and Crackers Wall Hanging gets students hooked on the Appli-Curves method and leaves them wanting to do more.

Cut the Fabrics

To begin the Cheese and Crackers Wall Hanging, cut:

- Two 8¾" (22cm) squares from red
- Two 8¾" (22cm) squares from dark gold
- Two 8¾" (22cm) squares from light gold
- Two 8¾" (22cm) squares from green
- Eight 8¾" (22cm) squares from black

Prepare the Heart Shapes

1 Print Template 13 from the CD. Trace 32 hearts onto the paper side of the fusible web, leaving at least 1" (3cm) between the pencil lines.

2 Cut out the shapes, leaving approximately ½" (1cm) extra outside of the pencil line. Trim the paper inside of the shape to approximately ⅛"–¼" (3mm–6mm) away from the pencil line.

Cut Out the Hearts

1 Follow manufacturer's instructions to fuse hearts onto the back of the remaining fabrics. Fuse:

- 4 on red
- 4 on dark gold
- 4 on light gold
- 4 on green
- 16 on black

2 Cut out each heart on the pencil line. Remove the paper strips from the back of each shape.

Make the Blocks

See Chapter 2 for basic block construction.

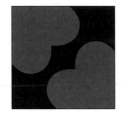

1 Fuse two black hearts onto each opposite corner of two red squares. Repeat for the dark gold, light gold and green squares, matching the sides and bottom of the shapes to the opposite corners of the squares. You will end up with two blocks with each colored background.

2 In the same way, fuse two red hearts onto each opposite corner of two black squares. Repeat for the dark gold hearts, light gold hearts and green hearts. You will end up with two blocks for each heart color.

3 Using thread to match the fused heart fabrics, stitch around the curved raw edges of the hearts.

4 On the back, trim away the background fabric so about ¼"–½" (6mm–13mm) remains by the stitching.

5 Using a rotary cutter and transparent ruler, cut the blocks once on the diagonal to bisect the hearts. Rearrange so a half-block is paired with its opposite-colored half-block. Using ¼" (6mm) seam allowances, stitch a center seam. Complete four units.

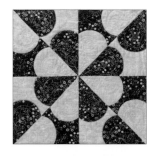
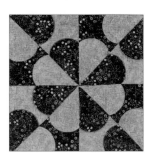

All blocks completed.

Completed block.

6 Arrange four same-colored units as shown to complete one block. There will be a lot of bulk where all the seams come together in the center. Consider pressing the seams in a clockwise spiral, or try pressing them open.

7 Complete three more blocks.

Finish the Wall Hanging

1   Lay out the blocks according to the diagram.

2   Join each row, and then join the rows to complete the quilt center. Press.

3   Use fabric-marking pencils to mark the top for quilting.

4   Layer the quilt top, batting and backing. Baste and quilt. Add binding to complete the wall hanging.

tip

This pattern makes a gorgeous four-block table runner as well. Just follow the instructions, but place the blocks in a diagonal row instead of a square.

Quilt layout diagram.

Center of quilt.

Quilting details.

A total of five circular motifs are created in this project: one in each of the four blocks and the fifth when the blocks are joined. Consider using a circular quilting design centered in these five motifs, as shown here.

NEW YORK BEAUTY:
YOU CAN DO IT!

Historically, the first New York Beauty blocks came into existence about 150–170 years ago. Also named the Rocky Mountain block according to some references, this block is a challenge since it merges spiky angles with curved piecing. A block any beginner would shy away from, it remains a favorite of many quilters around the globe. Dozens of variations of the New York Beauty have been sewn, and many are intricate and true works of art. In the projects that follow, the simplest version of New York Beauty is presented. And all the frustration is removed with the combination of two tricks: Paper-piecing and the Appli-Curves method assure even beginners amazing results. Never paper-pieced? Not to worry, I'll walk you through the steps, and you'll then finish off your block the Appli-Curves way. Simple, stunning and stress-free!

5

fans of lady liberty quilt

FINISHED QUILT SIZE: 62½" × 79½" (159CM × 202CM)

FINISHED BLOCK SIZE: 6" (15CM) SQUARE

UNFINISHED BLOCK SIZE: 6½" (17CM) SQUARE

NUMBER OF BLOCKS: 59

TEMPLATES NEEDED: OUTER ARC (TEMPLATE 16) OR OUTER ARC METHOD 2 (TEMPLATE 16-2), INNER ARC (TEMPLATE 17) OR INNER ARC METHOD 2 (TEMPLATE 17-2), AND PAPER-PIECED ARC (TEMPLATE 18). FOR METHOD 2, ADD: NEW YORK BEAUTY METHOD 2 (TEMPLATE 19)

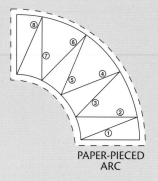

PAPER-PIECED ARC

For Method 1:

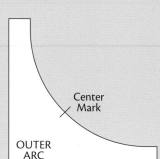

OUTER ARC — Center Mark

INNER ARC — Center Mark

For Method 2:

INNER ARC METHOD 2

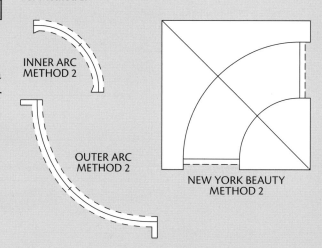

OUTER ARC METHOD 2

NEW YORK BEAUTY METHOD 2

In a stunning combination of deep, rich, hand-dyed fabrics, the New York Beauty block set on point creates a striking design. The setting is a great way for a beginner to use the Appli-Curves method on New York Beauty, since the blocks on point leave no seams to match with other blocks!

Cut the Fabrics

To begin the Fans of Lady Liberty Quilt, cut:

- Twelve 2" × 5" (5cm × 13cm) rectangles from each fat quarter
- Six 3" × 5" (8cm × 13cm) rectangles from each fat quarter
- Two 7" (18cm) squares from each fat quarter
- Two 4" (10cm) squares from each fat quarter

- Two 9¾" (25cm) strips from rich blue; sub-cut into five 9¾" (25cm) squares, then sub-cut twice on the diagonal to yield 20 triangles
- Two 5⅛" (13cm) squares from rich blue; sub-cut once on the diagonal to yield four triangles
- Six 2½" (6cm) strips from gold
- Eight 8½" (22cm) strips from deep purple
- Eight 2¼" (6cm) strips from deep purple for the binding

Sort the Fabrics

1 Each cut-up fat quarter will make parts for two blocks. First, pull three 3" × 5" (8cm × 13cm) rectangles and two 2" × 5" (5cm × 13cm) rectangles from each of the cut-up fat quarters. Make two sets, and pin each set together. These are the backgrounds for the paper-pieced arcs.

2 Pull the remaining 2" × 5" (5cm × 13cm) rectangles (there will be eight), and pin two sets of four each. These are the spikes for the paper-pieced arcs.

3 Match up a background group with a complementary spikes group. Each pairing will create two blocks. Make 59 sets (one will be left over).

Make the Paper-Pieced Arcs

1 Print Template 18 from the CD. You will need a total of 59 templates. Cut the arcs just outside of the dotted lines.

2 Follow the instructions in Chapter 2 for paper-piecing, using the sets made in the previous section. Trim all patches on the dotted lines.

tip

This quilt was made from fat quarter packs from Starr Design Fabrics, a hand-dyed fabric company that does all their dying on site in northern California. Every time I see one of these packs, I am forced to touch the fabrics and can't wait to work them up in a quilt. I purchased two 20-piece fat quarter packs to begin the blocks in this quilt and then added some other Starr Designs hand-dyed pieces from my stash. I played with a lot of arrangements, but this "fan" setting was my favorite. Putting all these fabrics together makes for a stunning quilt. It would also look great in brights, pastels or even various shades of one color.

Try using jewel tones or pastels for a different look.

Make the Blocks

See Chapter 2 for basic block construction.

1 Print templates 16 and 17 for Method 1 (see page 34) or templates 16-2 and 17-2 for Method 2 (see page 36) from the CD. Trace 59 of each (using Method 1 or Method 2) onto the paper side of the fusible web, leaving at least ½" (1cm) extra between the pencil lines. Cut out the shapes, leaving approximately ¼" (6mm) outside of the pencil lines.

2 Fuse the outer arc shapes onto the back of the 7" (18cm) squares, and fuse the inner arcs onto the back of the 4" (10cm) squares, following the instructions for either Method 1 or Method 2.

3 Cut on the curved lines, cutting the squares into two pieces. Remove the paper backing, and fuse the arcs onto the paper-pieced sections, using a 7" (18cm) muslin square if you chose Method 1.

tip

This quilt is made using fat quarters. This is the perfect group project, since quilters can have a "fabric exchange" and share fat quarters to create their own assortments. For example, if there are 20 quilters in your group, have everyone bring 30 fat quarters cut from three different fabrics. Decide on a color scheme to be sure all the fabrics will work together, such as "jewel tones" or "blue batiks." Then, share your fat quarters, and you'll end up with a scrappy assortment.

4 Using invisible nylon or thread to match the fabrics, stitch over the curves. Use a 6½" (17cm) diagonal square ruler to square up each block to 6½" (17cm). Complete a total of 59 blocks.

Assemble the Top

1 Lay out the blocks and rich blue triangles as shown. Place the blocks as you like for a pleasing arrangement.

2 Sew each diagonal row, and then sew the rows together to complete the quilt center. Press.

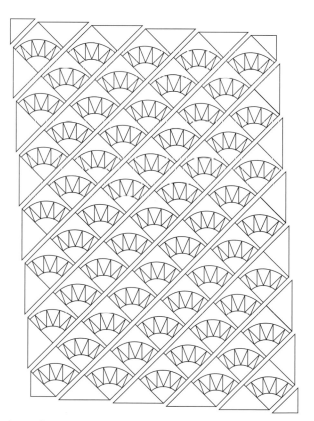

Layout diagram.

Add the Borders

1 Sew the gold and deep purple strips end-to-end with diagonal seams. Sub-cut the 2½" (6cm) gold strips into two 2½" × 60" (6cm × 152cm) strips for the sides and two 2½" × 47" (6cm × 119cm) strips for the top and bottom.

2 Sew the gold side borders, and then sew the top and bottom. Press.

3 Sub-cut the 8½" (22cm) deep purple strips into two 8½" × 64" (22cm × 163cm) strips for the sides and two 8½" × 63" (22cm × 160cm) strips for the top and bottom.

4 Sew the deep purple side borders, and then sew the top and bottom. Press.

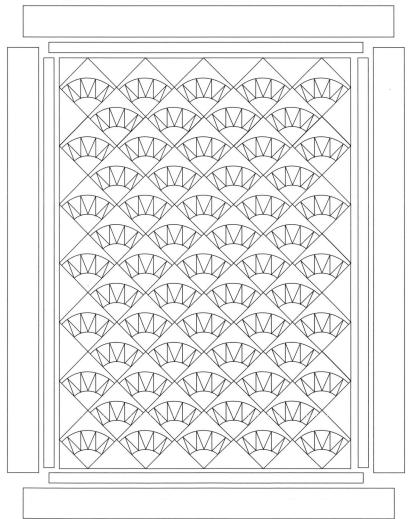

Sew the borders.

Finish the Quilt

1 Use fabric-marking pencils to mark the top for quilting.

Backing layout.

2 Remove the selvages from the backing fabric and cut three 40" × 83" (102cm × 211cm) rectangles. Seam as shown. Press.

3 Layer the quilt top, batting and backing. Baste and quilt. Add binding.

In keeping with the name of the block, machine quilter Val Sjoblom decided to quilt the Statue of Liberty and stars in the borders.

The star motif was repeated in the tops of the blocks to connect the border and block quilting.

united we stand quilt

MATERIALS

- ⅓ yd. (30cm) green stripe
- 1 yd. (.9m) green dot
- 1½ yd. (1.4m) gold dot
- 1½ yd. (1.4m) solid rust
- ⅔ yd. (60cm) brown paisley
- 1⅓ yd. (1.2m) natural plaid
- rust dot scraps
- rust plaid scraps
- 7" (18cm) muslin square (for Method 1 only)
- 56" x 56" (1.4m x 1.4m) square of batting
- 3¼ yd. (3m) fabric for backing
- 1 yd. (.9m) fabric for binding
- Paper-backed fusible web
- Thread to match fabrics

FINISHED QUILT SIZE: 52" (132CM) SQUARE

FINISHED BLOCK SIZE: 13½" (34CM)

UNFINISHED BLOCK SIZE: 14" (36CM)

NUMBER OF BLOCKS: 4

TEMPLATES NEEDED: OUTER ARC (TEMPLATE 16) OR OUTER ARC METHOD 2 (TEMPLATE 16-2), INNER ARC (TEMPLATE 17) OR INNER ARC METHOD 2 (17-2), PAPER-PIECED ARC (TEMPLATE 18), UNITED WE STAND STEM (TEMPLATE 20), UNITED WE STAND LEAF (TEMPLATE 21), UNITED WE STAND LARGE FLOWER (TEMPLATE 22), UNITED WE STAND SMALL FLOWER (TEMPLATE 23), UNITED WE STAND FLOWER CENTER (TEMPLATE 24). FOR METHOD 2, ADD: NEW YORK BEAUTY METHOD 2 (TEMPLATE 19)

This striking wall hanging combines many elements: blocks set on point, repeated sashing, appliquéd corners and even some interesting border effects. I've broken down all the steps—none are hard to do—so you can have your own stunning wall hanging in any color scheme that works for you!

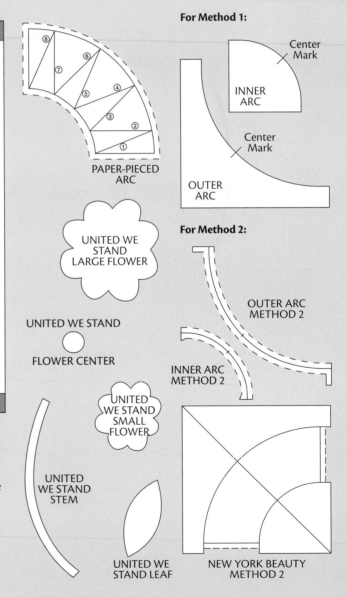

PAPER-PIECED ARC

For Method 1:

Center Mark

INNER ARC

Center Mark

OUTER ARC

UNITED WE STAND LARGE FLOWER

UNITED WE STAND FLOWER CENTER

For Method 2:

OUTER ARC METHOD 2

INNER ARC METHOD 2

UNITED WE STAND SMALL FLOWER

UNITED WE STAND STEM

UNITED WE STAND LEAF

NEW YORK BEAUTY METHOD 2

Cut the Fabrics

To begin the United We Stand Quilt, cut:

- Two 23" (58cm) squares from natural plaid; cut once on the diagonal to yield four triangles
- Thirty-two 2" × 5" (5cm × 13cm) rectangles from gold dot
- Forty-eight 3" × 5" (8cm × 13cm) rectangle from gold dot
- Sixty-four 2" × 5" (5cm × 13cm) rectangles rust fabric
- Four 2" (5cm) squares gold dot
- Sixteen 7" (18cm) squares green dot

- Sixteen 4" (10cm) squares green stripe
- Sixteen 2" × 6½" (5cm × 17cm) rectangles brown paisley
- Four 3½" × 14" (9cm × 36cm) rectangles rust fabric
- One 3½" (9cm) square from natural plaid
- Five 1" (3cm) strips from brown paisley
- Five 1¼" (3cm) strips from gold dot
- Six 4½" (11cm) strips from solid rust
- Six 2¼" (6cm) strips from solid rust for the binding

Make the Paper-Pieced Arcs

1 Print Template 18 from the CD. You will need a total of 16 templates. Cut the arcs just outside of the dotted lines.

2 Follow the instructions in Chapter 2 for paper-piecing, using gold dot 3" × 5" (8cm × 13cm) and 2" × 5" (5cm × 13cm) rectangles, and solid rust 2" × 5" (5cm × 13cm) rectangles for the spikes.

3 Trim all of the paper-pieced sections on the dotted lines.

Make the Blocks

See Chapter 2 for basic block construction.

1 Print templates 16 and 17 for Method 1 (see page 34) or 16-2 and 17-2 for Method 2 (see page 36). Trace 16 of each, using Method 1 or Method 2, onto the paper side of the fusible web. Leave at least ½" (1cm) extra between the pencil lines.

2 Cut out the shapes, leaving approximately ¼" (6mm) outside the pencil lines.

3 Fuse the outer arc shapes onto the back of the 7" (18cm) green dot squares, and the inner arcs onto the back of the 4" (10cm) green stripe squares, following instructions for the method that you have chosen from Chapter 2.

4 Cut on the curved lines, cutting the squares into two pieces.

5 Remove the paper backing.

6 Fuse the arcs onto the paper-pieced sections, using a 7" (18cm) muslin square if you chose Method 1.

7 Using invisible nylon or thread to match the fabrics, stitch the curves.

Make 16.

8 Using 6½" (17cm) diagonal square ruler, square up each block to 6½" (17cm). Complete a total of 16 units.

Make 4.

9 Lay out four units, four 2" × 6½" (5cm × 17cm) brown paisley rectangles, and a 2" (5cm) gold dot square as shown to complete a block. Piece each row, and then join the rows.

Assemble the Top

1 Lay out the blocks, 3½" × 14" (9cm × 36cm) solid rust rectangles and 3½" (9cm) natural plaid square as shown. Piece each row, then join the rows.

2 Attach 23" (58cm) natural plaid triangles to each side. These triangles will be larger than needed, and will be cut down later.

3 Print templates 20–24 from the CD. Trace 12 large flowers, 12 small flowers, 12 flower centers, 4 stems and 21 leaf shapes onto the paper side of fusible web, leaving at least ½" (1cm) extra between the pencil lines.

4 Fuse the shapes onto the back of the fabric indicated below. Fuse:

- 2 large flowers on the brown paisley, 4 on the solid rust, 4 on the rust dot and 2 on the rust plaid

- 3 small flowers on the brown paisley, 4 on the solid rust, 3 on the rust dot and 2 on the rust plaid
- 12 flower centers on the gold dot
- 11 leaf shapes on the green dot and 10 on the green stripe
- 2 stems on the green dot and 2 on the green stripe

5 Lay out the appliqué shapes as shown. Remember to leave room for the seam allowances by the edges. Fuse the shapes on the quilt top. Using thread to match the appliqué, stitch around the raw edges of the shapes.

Quilt top layout, showing appliqué placement.

6 Trim the natural plaid triangles so ½" (1cm) extends beyond the outer points of the center patchwork.

117

Add the Borders

1 Join the brown paisley strips end-to-end with
diagonal seams. Press lengthwise with wrong
sides together. Cut into four 42¾" (109cm) segments.

Attach brown paisley to each raw edge.

2 Pin the brown paisley strips on the edges of the
quilt, with raw edges matching. Stitch with a ¼"
(6mm) seam.

3 Join the 1¼" (3cm) gold dot strips end to end
with diagonal seams. Sub-cut into two 1¼" ×
42¾" (3cm × 109cm) and two 1¼" × 44¼" (3cm ×
112cm) strips.

4 Sew the 1¼" (3cm) gold dot segments to opposite sides, and then remaining sides. Press.

5 Join the 4½" (11cm) solid rust strips end-to-end
with diagonal seams. Sub-cut into two 4½" × 44¼"
(11cm × 112cm) and two 4½" × 52¼" (11cm × 133cm)
strips.

Attach the border.

6 Attach the 4½" (11cm) rust fabric segments to
opposite sides, and then remaining sides. Press.

Finish the Quilt

1 Mark the top for quilting, using fabric-marking pencils.

Backing layout.

2 Remove the selvages from the backing fabric and cut into two 40" × 57" (102cm × 145cm) rectangles. Seam as shown. Press.

3 Layer the quilt top, batting and backing. Baste and quilt. Add binding.

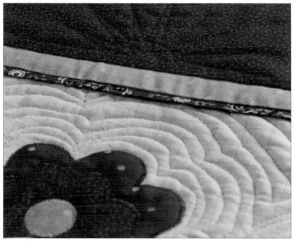

Stitching details.

crowned jewels quilt

MATERIALS

- 3¼ yd. (2.9m) black print, including binding
- 4¼ yd. (3.9m) red print
- 1½ yd. (1.4m) blue print
- 2⅔ yd. (2.4m) purple print
- 1 yd. (.9m) cream print
- 3⅓ yd. (3m) green stripe*
- 85" × 101" (216cm x 257cm) rectangle of batting

- 3¼ yd. (3m) fabric for backing
- Paper-backed fusible web
- Thread to match fabrics
- 7" (18cm) muslin square
  (for Method 1 only)

* Although a stripe was used for the green, any
  solid or print fabric can be substituted.

FINISHED QUILT SIZE: 62½" × 79½"
  (159CM X 202CM)
FINISHED BLOCK SIZE: 6" (15CM) SQUARE
UNFINISHED BLOCK SIZE: 6½" (17CM) SQUARE
NUMBER OF BLOCKS: 59
TEMPLATES NEEDED: OUTER ARC (TEMPLATE 16)
  OR OUTER ARC METHOD 2 (TEMPLATE 16-2),
  INNER ARC (TEMPLATE 17) OR INNER ARC
  METHOD 2 (TEMPLATE 17-2), AND PAPER-
  PIECED ARC (TEMPLATE 18). FOR METHOD
  2, ADD: NEW YORK BEAUTY METHOD 2
  (TEMPLATE 19)

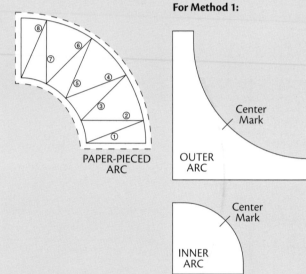

PAPER-PIECED
ARC

For Method 1:

OUTER
ARC

Center
Mark

INNER
ARC

Center
Mark

For Method 2:

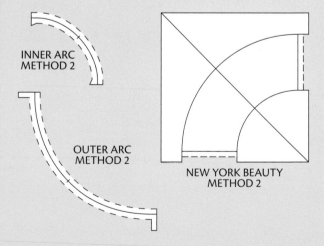

INNER ARC
METHOD 2

OUTER ARC
METHOD 2

NEW YORK BEAUTY
METHOD 2

The deep rich colors used in this quilt create a striking
design, set off by the light "crosses" in each of the large
blocks. The unusual border corners also add interest
and carry out the design of the quilt center.

Cut the Fabrics

To begin the New York Beauty blocks, cut:

- Nineteen 5" (13cm) purple strips; sub-cut into 368 rectangles 2" × 5" (5cm × 13cm) for spikes
- Thirty 5" (13cm) red strips; sub-cut into 184 rectangles 2" × 5" (5cm × 13cm) and 276 rectangles 3" × 5" (8cm × 13cm)
- One 1½" (4cm) black strip

- Ten 4" (10cm) blue strips; sub-cut into 92 squares 4" (10cm) wide
- Seventeen 7" (18cm) green stripe strips; sub-cut into 92 squares 7" (18cm) wide
- Four 6½" (17cm) cream strips; sub-cut into 44 rectangles 1½" × 6½" (4cm × 17cm) (two strips will remain uncut)

For sashing and cornerstones, cut:

- Seventeen 3½" (9cm) black strips; sub-cut into 49 rectangles 3½" × 13½" (9cm × 34cm)
- Four 3½" (9cm) blue strips; sub-cut into 30 squares 3½" (9cm) wide

For borders and binding, cut:

- Five 1½" (4cm) cream strips
- Four 6½" (17cm) black strips
- Ten 2½" (6cm) black strips for binding

tip

These fabrics are from my From the Attic line by Andover Fabrics. I had a lot of fun with them, especially the green stripe, which was placed in such a way to move the eye around the block. This creates a subtle interest that may not be noticed at first.

Make the Paper-Pieced Arcs

1 Print Template 18 from the CD. You will need a total of 92 templates. Cut the arcs just outside of the dotted lines.

2 Follow the instructions in Chapter 2 for paper-piecing, using the 3" × 5" (8cm × 13cm) and 2" × 5" (5cm × 13cm) red rectangles for the background and the 2" × 5" (5cm × 13cm) purple rectangles for the spikes.

3 Trim all paper-pieced sections on the dotted lines.

Make the New York Beauty Units

See Chapter 2 for basic block construction.

1 Print templates 16 and 17 for Method 1 (see page 34) or 16-2 and 17-2 for Method 2 (see page 36). Trace 92 of each shape (using Method 1 or Method 2) onto the paper side of the fusible web, leaving at least ½" (1cm) between the pencil lines. Cut out the shapes, leaving approximately ¼" (6mm) extra outside of the pencil lines.

2 Fuse the outer arc shapes onto the back of the 7" (18cm) green stripe squares and the inner arcs onto the back of the 4" (10cm) blue squares. Follow instructions for the method that you have chosen.

3 Cut on the curved lines, cutting the squares into two pieces. Remove the paper backing.

4 Fuse the arcs onto the paper-pieced sections, using a 7" (18cm) muslin square if you chose Method 1.

5 Stitch the curves using invisible nylon or thread to match the fabrics.

Make 92.

6 Use a 6½" (17cm) diagonal square ruler to square up each block to 6½" (17cm). Complete 92 units.

Make the Large Blocks

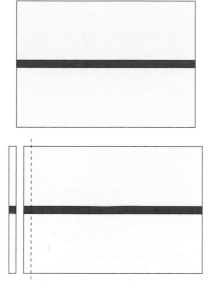

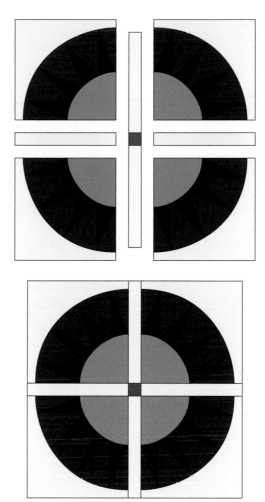

Make 20.

1 Stitch two 6½" (17cm) cream strips and one 1½" (4cm) black strip as shown. Sub-cut the three pieces crosswise into twenty 1½" (4cm) segments.

tip

Notice that the blocks are the same as the blocks used in the United We Stand Quilt *on page 114. By using different fabric scales and color, the block takes on a whole different look. The colors of the "spikes" and "background" of the New York Beauty blocks in the* Crowned Jewels Quilt *are similar in value, so the spikes are not as prominent, resulting in a different look. Be sure to consider color and color value when selecting your fabrics to obtain the look you desire.*

2 Lay out one segment from the previous step, four New York Beauty units, and two 1½" × 6½" (4cm × 17cm) cream rectangles as shown to complete a large block. Piece each row, and then join the rows.

Note: You will have twelve New York Beauty units and four 1½" × 6½" (4cm × 17cm) cream rectangles left over, which will be used on the borders.

Assemble the Top

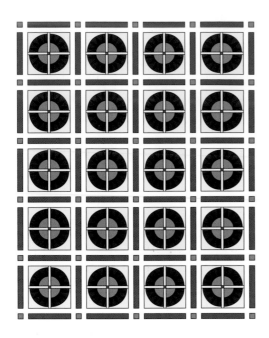

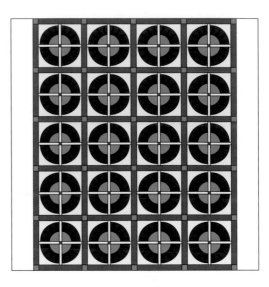

1 Lay out the blocks, 3½" × 13½" (9cm × 34cm) black rectangles, and 3½" (9cm) blue squares as shown. Piece each row, and then join the rows to complete the quilt center.

2 Join the remaining 1½" (4cm) cream strips end-to-end with a diagonal seam. Press. Join the 6½" (17cm) black strips end-to-end with a straight seam. Press.

3 Sub-cut two 1½" × 83½" (4cm × 212cm) cream strips for the sides and two 1½" × 81½" (4cm × 207cm) cream strips for the top and bottom. Sub-cut two 6½" × 71½" (17cm × 182cm) black strips for the sides and two 6½" × 55½" (17cm × 141cm) black strips for the top and bottom.

4 Sew the 83½" (212cm) cream segments to the sides of the quilt center.

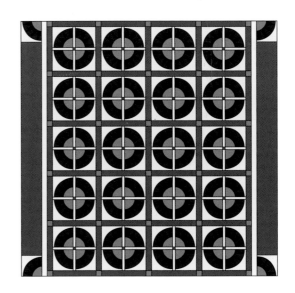

5 Sew one 6" (15cm) New York Beauty block to each end of each 71½" (182cm) black segment, in the orientation shown. Attach to the sides of the quilt center.

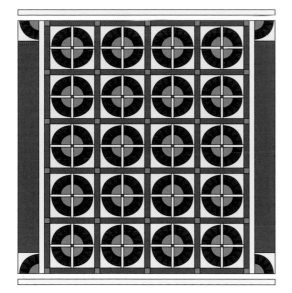

6 Sew the 81½" (207cm) cream segments to the top and bottom of the quilt.

7 Join two New York Beauty blocks and two 1½" × 6½" (4cm × 17cm) cream rectangles to each 55½" (141cm) black segment as shown. Sew this segment to the top and bottom of the quilt center to complete the quilt top.

Finish the Quilt

1 Use fabric-marking pencils to mark the top for quilting.

Backing layout.

2 Remove the selvages from the backing fabric, and cut into three 40" × 85" (102cm × 216cm) rectangles. Seam as shown. Press.

3 Layer the quilt top, batting and backing. Baste and quilt.

4 Add binding.

resources

Andover Fabrics

1384 Broadway, Suite 1500
New York, NY 10018
(800) 223-5678
andoverfabrics.com

Bear Thread Designs

P.O. Box 1452
Highlands, TX 77562
(281) 462-0661
bearthreaddesigns.com
Appliqué-pressing sheet

Bernina of America, Inc.

3702 Prairie Lake Ct.
Aurora, IL 60504
(630) 978-2500
berninausa.com
Sewing machines

The Quilted Closet, Inc.

6651 NW 48th St.
Johnston, IA 50131
(515) 270-6238
thequiltedcloset.com
Quilting patterns and accessories

Starr Design Fabrics, Inc.

P.O. Box 440
Etna, CA 96027
(530) 467-5121
starrfabrics.com

Superior Threads

87 East 2580 South
St. George, UT 84790
(800) 499-1777
superiorthreads.com

Therm O Web Adhesives

770 Glenn Ave.
Wheeling, IL 60090
(800) 323-0799
thermowebonline.com
HeatnBond Lite

Val Sjoblom

On A Wing & A Prayer
2717 Crescent Dr.
International Falls, MN 56649
(218) 285-9962
onawingquilting.com
Quality, custom machine quilting

index

think outside the block

Spinning Pinwheel Quilts:

Easy Piecing Using the 3-6-9 Design System

by Sara Moe

Using the fun, pinless and foolproof 3-6-9 Design System, you'll discover endless quilt design possibilities within your reach. Includes bonus CD featuring appliqué templates and embroidery designs. *Paperback, 8¼ × 10⅞, 128 p, 225 color photos,* **ISBN-13: 978-0-89689-559-1, ISBN-10: 0-89689-559-9,** *Item# Z0996*

Designing Patchwork on Your Computer

by Carol Phillipson

This book/CD combination provides you with step-by-step instructions for designing a wide range of patchwork blocks, using just a few keystrokes. *Hardcover, 8¼ × 9¼, 128 p, 400 color photos and illustrations,* **ISBN-13:978-0-89689-400-6, ISBN-10: 0-89689-400-2,** *Item# Z0755*

Log Cabin Quilts with Attitude:

A New Twist on an Old Favorite

by Sharon Rotz

Discover a new twist on traditional quilting, and showcase individuality with the clever "freedom block" approach demonstrated in 15 step-by-step projects, 300 color photos and appliqué patterns. *Paperback, 8¼ × 10⅞, 128 p, 275+ color photos and illustrations,* **ISBN-13: 978-0-89689-308-5, ISBN-10: 0-89689-308-1,** *Item# LCQA*

Tessellation Quilts:

Sensational Designs from Interlocking Patterns

by Christine Porter

Discover the rewards of learning to translate an ancient pattern into beautiful pieced patchwork designs in this exciting book, which turns an interesting mathematical phenomenon into a beautiful quilt design. *Paperback, 8¼ × 10⅞, 128 p, 200 color photos & 100 illustrations,* **ISBN-13: 978-0-7153-1941-3, ISBN-10: 0-7153-1941-8,** *Item# 41865*

Traditional Quilts with a Twist:

Exciting New Looks for your Favorite Patterns

by Maggie Ball

Use traditional quilt blocks to create unique variations through more than 20 projects demonstrated in 200+ color photos. *Paperback, 8¼ × 10⅞, 128 p, 200+ color photos and illustrations,* **ISBN-13: 978-0-89689-273-6, ISBN-10: 0-89689-273-5,** *Item# TRQV*

Discover imagination,
innovation and inspiration at
www.mycraftivity.com.
Connect. Create. Explore.